Social Life in Ireland 1800-45

Edited by
R. B. McDOWELL

Published for
The Cultural Relations Committee
of Ireland
by the Mercier Press,
4 Bridge Street, Cork.

SBN 85342 295 8
First Edition 1957
Reprinted 1963,
1973

THE aim of this series is to give a broad, informed survey of Irish life and culture, past and present. Each writer is left free to deal with his subject in his own way, and the views expressed are not necessarily those of the Committee. The general editor of the series is Caoimhín Ó Danachair.

PRINTED IN THE REPUBLIC OF IRELAND BY
LEINSTER LEADER LTD., NAAS, CO. KILDARE

CONTENTS

LIST OF ILLUSTRATIONS

PREFACE

In Ireland the nineteenth century began with the act of union and was bisected by the Famine. The former marked the end of the Anglo-Irish constitutional experiment of 1782, the latter resulted from the collapse of the Irish agrarian system. It is then tempting to dismiss the whole half century as an era characterised by disappointment, lost opportunities, waste and dissension, a fitting prelude to the great catastrophe which terminates it. And to some extent this attitude is justifiable. During quarter of a century political energy and intelligence were largely absorbed in the long drawn out exacerbating struggle for complete Catholic emancipation. During the whole fifty years sectarian strife was rife, invading and poisoning a surprising number of issues. The Repeal agitation and the Young Ireland movement failed hopelessly. O'Connell died worn out and disappointed, the Young Irelanders were defeated and scattered in exile. Yet an intelligent unionist must have been disturbed by the failure of the union to win hearty general acceptance. Over most of the country social conditions were deplorable, agriculture stagnated and industry decayed. Such a system afforded a poor livelihood and a precarious support to a steadily increasing population while breeding a wide variety of social tensions. Moreover the factors governing the major Irish problems seemed to be arranged with a perverse intricacy calculated to baffle the well-intentioned and sensible reformer.

But it would be a mistake to dwell exclusively on the dark side of the picture. The nineteenth century was a progressive and vigorous age and Ireland was bound to share in the tendencies of the time. And Irish problems by their very complexity and magnitude were a stimulus to thought and action. Under the pressure of circumstances novel methods of political organization were evolved, the technique of social investigation greatly developed, political ideas were freshly examined, the educational system expanded, and a modern civil service tradition built up. Also religion which loomed so large in the life of the time meant more than inter-denominational controversy. In each of the principal Irish religious bodies there were significant developments. The Catholics, relieved from the pressure of the penal laws, were busy with the task of ecclesiastical rehabilitation. Churches were being built all over the country, new orders were founded, the educational and charitable efforts of the church extended. In the Protestant churches the evangelical revival produced a sense of urgency and responsibility which expressed itself in much more individual and corporate effort.

Though theology and politics were the staple debate in Ireland at this time, intellectual life was lively and productive in many other directions. It was the great age of Irish mathematics and medicine. And if it would be foolish to make exaggerated claims for the literary tradition represented by Maria Edgeworth, Carleton, Maginn, Lever and Ferguson, it at least can be said that a reasonable proportion of their very prolific output deserves to survive. Finally we still possess many survivals of the architecture of the period which continued with taste and courage the eighteenth century tradition.

The eight essays which make up this work, were broadcast by Radio Eireann between 14 February and 4 April 1955, as a series of Thomas Davis lectures. They do not attempt to provide a comprehensive survey of this highly complex era. Instead, by selecting some interesting and significant aspects of the period, they make it possible for the reader to approach it from several different angles, and so gain at least a general impression of the vigour and variety of social life in Ireland at this time.

I

DUBLIN AND BELFAST —
A COMPARISON

BY R. B. MCDOWELL

THE FIRST OF January, 1801—the first day of the nineteenth century was a momentous date in Dublin history. For on that day the city ceased to be the parliamentary capital of a theoretically independent state and became the second city of the United Kingdom. The eighteenth century of course had been Dublin's great age. Then it had been the political and social centre of a proud, self-confident ascendancy which was enjoying with few qualms the fruits of victory. Moreover, during the last two decades of the century, the constitutional changes which had raised Ireland's status, gave protestant Ireland and to some extent the whole country, a fresh infusion of self-confidence, and this was reflected in Dublin by a great outburst of building which produced streets and squares of large mansions and the two great administrative edifices, the Four Courts and the Custom House, which still dominate the Liffey. During the parliamentary session three hundred commoners and about eighty peers were resident in Dublin and to the interest and excitement aroused by politics was added all the gaiety generated by a vigorous social programme. The aspect and spirit of pre-union Dublin both are preserved for us in the well known series of prints by Malton, completed in 1791, which show a stately classical capital endowed with a grave, almost melancholy self-conscious dignity. By a fortunate chance we have also another set of prints for post-union Dublin, those produced by Brocas about 1818 which provide an effective and significant contrast to Malton's. In Brocas' prints the buildings still stand almost unaltered, but they are simply a background to the bustling, crowded, coloursome life of the streets. Dublin as seen by Brocas is clearly an important, cheerful, vivacious if a trifle vulgar, provincial city. And the dawn of a new era is aptly emphasised by the fact that the Custom House provides a background to the long funnel of a paddle steamer.

In spite of its fall in status and the material losses caused by the union, Dublin during the early 19th century was an expanding and lively place. Admittedly there were depressing changes. The parliament house was the Bank of Ireland, and several of the large urban mansions had—anticipating a process which was to occur all over Europe during the next century and a half—become public offices and institutions. By 1830 Powerscourt House was the Stamp Office, Aldborough House was an experimental school, Leinster House was the headquarters of the Royal Dublin Society, and Moira House the Mendicity Institute. And by then Dublin had less than a score of resident peers. With the disappearance of the Irish parliament the professional classes tended to predominate in Dublin society. Indeed it was pointed out that after the union even city tradesmen were managing to get received at the Viceregal court. But it was argued that if this showed a shocking decline in social standards it at least added a courtly polish to Dublin business life.

Throughout the nineteenth century Dublin remained a commercial, administrative, military, educational, theological, economic and political centre of no mean importance. Between 1801 and 1841, the population grew from about 172,000 to 230,000. And there is plenty of architectural evidence of the city's growth. The Post Office, the Pro-Cathedral, the King's Inns, St. George's with a steeple which is probably the finest in Ireland the Castle Chapel, and the College of Surgeons, are all post-union. Moreover, during the first half of the nineteenth century block after block of respectable, flat fronted brick houses, placed in uniform rows filled up the area between the great eighteenth century squares, Stephen's Green and Merrion Square and the Grand Canal while northwards the city advanced less quickly beyond Mountjoy Square and along the Circular Road. Here and there the advance can be dated by the naming of streets after viceroys. Hardwicke, Richmond, Whitworth, Talbot, Northumberland, Haddington, Heytesbury, Bessborough, are all nineteenth century viceroys commemorated in this way. Not only were the areas between the canals filled in but neat villas and sedate terraces spread along the coast stretching southwards as far as the newly named Kingstown which in 1830 was linked to Dublin by the first Irish Railway.

In another respect Dublin showed continued and increased vitality after the union. Cultural life was exceedingly active. The *Comet*, a waspish radical journal, and later the far more generous *Nation* provided stimulating rallying points for reformers and nationalists, and for the Conservatives the *Dublin University Magazine* formed a similar centre. Understandably in a country racked by controversy, politics was the main *raison d'etre* of these journals, but in the Dublin of Lady Morgan, Mangan, Maturin, William Hamilton, Petrie and Lever, intellectual interests far transcended mere party warfare. It was the great age of Dublin mathematics and the foundations were being laid of modern Celtic studies. There is not a simple explanation for this intellectual exuberance. Dublin was certainly affected by the major currents in contemporary European thought; political excitement (of which there was plenty) probably acted as a stimulant; and finally Dublin was one of the great educational centres in the British Isles. Visitors to Ireland at this time continually speak of the determination with which the middle classes emphasised their gentility. And, as in any case over most of Ireland industry was languishing, necessity as well as snobbery frequently weighted the balance in favour of a profession when the choice of a career was n question.

During the first half of the nineteenth century Trinity College enjoyed a boom which was permanently marked by the building of Botany Bay and New Square. For the training of medical men Dublin had particularly good facilities since benevolence taking an obvious course had amply endowed the city with hospitals. And in addition to the university medical school, there was the College of Surgeons and a number of private medical Schools. These private schools, which prepared their pupils for the examinations of the licensing bodies, were started by enterprising groups of medical men who depended on their reputation and teaching abilities to attract pupils. One such group was careful to build its school in the style of a methodist meeting house so that they could dispose of it easily in the event of the school proving a failure. And the place which Dublin held in medicine at this time is still grimly commemorated in medical nomenclature by Colles' fracture and Graves' disease.

Important as the Dublin medical world was it was surpassed at least numerically by the legal, for while there were in Dublin at the census of 1841, 700 medical men, there were no fewer than 1,900 lawyers, a total made up of ten judges, 400 barristers and 1,500 attorneys. Only one great jurist sat on the Irish bench during this period, Sugden, now usually remembered for the muddle he made over his own will. But the Irish Bar had a great reputation for eloquence. A reputation fostered by Bushe, Curran, O'Connell and Plunket, and continued amongst the younger men, by Napier, Whiteside and Butt. Admittedly an acid critic suggested that much of the eloquence was due to the fact that business being not so brisk as in London Irish barristers were able to indulge in the universal human desire to talk at length. The works of Phillips and Barrington are probably the best known sources of Irish legal life at this time, and show it as a series of skirmishes won by luck or audacity, and their Irish barrister as a blend of the cavalier and the lawyer, ready to use his pistols as well as the year-books. But both Barrington and Phillips were out to entertain their readers, they were both hard up, their style is forced and exaggerated, and their books crammed with that legendary gossip in which historic fact gets buried beneath masses of anecdotal embellishment. But even from the day to day evidence of the contemporary press it is clear that litigation was often fascinating and exciting and on an occasion such as O'Connell's trial in 1844, the manoeuvring, oratory, drama and comedy of the courts surpassed anything that could be provided by the theatre.

Law and politics were of course closely connected. Partly because political issues frequently emerged as legal cases, and partly because most of the leading political figures were barristers. Irish politics at this time affected Dublin intimately and directly in three ways. Firstly all nation-wide movements tended to centre there, secondly as a result of the great shift in the Irish social balance which is marked in the statute book by the Catholic Relief Act of 1829, Dublin began to change from a predominantly protestant to a predominantly Catholic city. Even in the early nineteenth century over seventy per cent of the population of Dublin were Catholics. But protestantism greatly predominated in the more influential walks of life and it was bound to be a long time before the full results of the relief act were apparent. The most discernible sign of the improvement in the Catholic position during the early years of the century were the new Catholic churches. During the eighteenth century Catholic places of worship had been small and inconspicuous, indeed almost hidden. The emergence of the Irish Catholics from their catacombs and their renewed self-confidence were symbolised by the opening of the Pro-Cathedral in 1816. Though even then it was cautiously placed just a little back from the great central thoroughfare. A number of new Catholic parish churches followed, on one of which, St. Andrew's, Westland Row, was placed the first large statue publicly displayed on a Catholic Church in Dublin. And in 1841 a Catholic, Daniel O'Connell was chosen as Lord Mayor by the corporation set up under the Irish municipal Reform Act of 1840. The creation of this body was the result of the reform movement which during the first half of the nineteenth century was responsible for drastically remodelling on rational lines so many institutions. At the beginning of the nineteenth century the Dublin Corporation which was largely responsible for the government of the city was remarkable for its antiquity and inefficiency. It consisted of a Lord Mayor, two sheriffs, a board of aldermen, the members of which were chosen for life largely by co-option, and the Commons, made up of ninety-six representatives of

16

View from Carlisle Bridge

DUBLIN

Published Feb.y 1.st 1820 by The Print the Best of Price of DUBLIN or 201 aged Charles & & Moules & Hill Tails Street Bloomsbury London

D'OLIER STREET AND WESTMORELAND STREET, DUBLIN

the guilds; these guilds of which there were, in 1830 twenty, were mainly medieval in origin and theoretically were composed of persons engaged in the various trades. In fact they had lost almost all connection with the business life of the city and were political clubs, rigorously protestant and conservative in outlook, which scrutinized severely the political and theological credentials of anyone who wanted to join them. The corporation had a large staff of picturesque officials but many of its obvious functions were being performed by other *ad hoc* bodies set up by acts of parliament. The most controversial of these was the Dublin police establishment which was under the control of magistrates appointed partly by the corporation and partly by the government. The police establishment was certainly costly but about 1830 it was said there were too few day police and the night watchmen were so old and decrepit that an experienced magistrate would not muster them in daylight. Then there was the ballast board responsible for the harbour and the paving board nominated by the central government which looked after the surfacing of the streets. It managed to accomplish a good deal of work but its members were twice discovered to be misapplying funds. Lastly there was the Wide Streets Commission, also nominated by the Government, which was still busy during the early nineteenth century buying land and directing urban development. The archaic and complex nature of Dublin's administration was emphasised by the existence of the three Liberties, which covered an area to the South West of the city which was for many municipal and legal purposes excluded from the jurisdiction of the corporation. I may add that in the small Liberty of St. Patrick's which covered about five acres in the shadow of the Cathedral, all machinery for enforcing the collection of small debts had decayed and vanished so it had become a local Alsatia.

By the beginning of the thirties then the Dublin Corporation was doubly obnoxious to liberals. It was a clumsy body which performed its duties badly, and it was composed of fervent conservatives who proclaimed their allegiance at city dinners and elsewhere and monopolised the prizes and perquisites of civic government. In 1833 the liberal attack opened by the appointment of commissioners to enquire into the working of the Irish corporations, and the report on Dublin which fills a volume was an objective recital of the damning facts. Still the local conservatives were unabashed, and though their parliamentary chiefs displayed moderated enthusiasm in their defence, they fought hard. But by 1840 they were defeated and the medieval corporation was replaced by a new functional body elected by the ratepayers which during the next decade absorbed all the normal duties of civic government.

In one respect Dublin was unfortunate during this period. It was one of those urban centres which failed to profit proportionately by the industrial revolution. It remained of course a great port, but industries showed little vitality and the liberties the traditional home of the city's textile industries contained large depressed areas. Whitelaw, a pioneer in social statistics, paints a gloomy picture of the network of lanes, alleys, courts, dark, filthy, overcrowded and disease-ridden, badly drained, with too many dram shops, where craftsmen belonging to a past era were exposed to the fluctuating blasts of economic adversity.

Belfast formed a complete contrast to Dublin—if Dublin could claim to be a medieval city. Belfast at the beginning of the seventeenth century had been a village.

Dublin during the eighteenth century had been a sumptuous capital, Belfast had only been a remote provincial town. But towards the close of the century it was being realised that Belfast, though a provincial town was at least a distinctive one. And the Duke of Rutland making a vice-regal progress in 1787, referred to it as a giant town. Now as the population of Belfast at the end of the eighteenth century was probably under 20,000—that is to say, about an eighth that of Dublin, the Duke could not have been thinking in terms of sheer size. What he was talking about was the speed at which the town was growing. By 1850 it had quintupled itself and had 100,000 inhabitants. Now as Belfast, unlike Dublin, was of little or no administrative importance—it was not even a country town—its growth was obviously caused by economic factors. At the beginning of the nineteenth century it had been for some generations the great marketing centre of the Ulster Linen industry. The linen industry was fortunate for it enjoyed through the eighteenth century government patronage, being regarded in official quarters as Ireland's natural, indeed almost predestined, contribution to the imperial economy. Moreover up in Ulster spinning and weaving was carried on in the homes of a sturdy peasantry, whose self-reliance was often nourished by non-conformity and securely rooted in the customs which protected them in their dealings with their landlords. Eastern Ulster and particularly the Lagan valley was a rich and active zone, and Belfast, concentrated round the Lagan mouth and, clamped firmly in place by the great cliff-like hill which rears up to the north west of the town, had developed into the economic centre of the region. Architecturally it has to be admitted it was a very ordinary town. At the beginning of the nineteenth century it still clustered round

High Street and Hercules Street and even in the forties it was only beginning to straggle out southwards from the Great Northern Railway station opened in the early forties, to the new Queen's College which was finished in 1849. And while there were some terraces of plain high brick houses for the more prosperous citizens, a few of which survive in the centre of the city, the bulk of the town was composed of a maze of short narrow undistinguished streets of small houses unrelieved by any great public buildings. There were of course a number of churches, modelled on classical temples, the most striking being perhaps the Chapel of Ease to the Parish Church of St. Anne, which owed its portico to a curious accident. The pillars had in fact belonged to a mansion built by the magnificent and eccentric Bishop of Derry, and when it was pulled down the pillars were brought to Belfast and stuck on the church. St. Anne's itself it may be added, had a flamboyant steeple which impressed even a Dublin visitor. Significantly enough, the finest building in the town was the Linenhall which dominated Belfast, standing in the centre of the principal square. It was a large brick block, restrained and even elegant with its pedamented entrance, and it provided a number of booths where linen merchants could carry on their trade. Its presence was a continuous reminder of the importance of linen to Belfast and Ulster. Though as a matter of fact at the beginning of the nineteenth century it seemed as if linen even in the north of Ireland was going to be overshadowed by the typical textile industry of the new era—cotton. Enterprising Belfast business men were quick to see the profitable opportunities it offered for the employment of the capital, skill and labour force they could deploy. The raw material was imported and cotton factories sprang up, and Mrs. Hall, the famous literary tourist was able to call Belfast the Irish Manchester. Though she tactfully explained that the Belfast air was purified by fresh sea breezes. This phase in Belfast's economic life lasted only for a generation. For rapid and ruinous price fluctuations and the strength of British competition turned Belfast manufacturers away from cotton back to the firmly grounded linen industry. But the short lived cotton era left its mark on the town's industrial life. Its leaders had been unhindered by tradition and had been ready to adopt up-to-date ideas—including the factory and steam power. Factories with their regular hours and discipline were highly unpopular among the northern operatives, who called them lock-ups. But they had obvious advantages from the employers point of view and by the middle of the century there were a number of linen factories in Belfast. In addition to being a manufacturing centre Belfast was also a port, being the second in Ireland. This was largely due to the persevering and intelligent enterprise of its merchants. Though they had the Lagan and the Lough the approach to the harbour was shallow, narrow and twisted. During the eighteenth century a little was done to improve matters but it was in the thirties, after prolonged negotiations with vested interests, tiresome efforts to raise the necessary funds and disputes between engineering experts, that the new cut which immensely improved the channel was made and the modern system of docks begun. While the port was developing shipbuilding was not unnaturally growing in importance and in 1820 the first Belfast built steam boat was launched just a year after the first cross-channel steam boat service based on Belfast was started.

It would be a mistake however to regard Belfast merely as a successful money making hive. Its citizens indeeed prided themselves on the vigour and variety of their intellectual interests. The number of learned societies the town possessed at the opening of the nineteenth century was remarkable. There was the Literary Society, the Historical Society (a debating club), the Anecreonic Society, the Belfast Natural History Society, and the Belfast Society for Promoting Knowledge, whose first librarian was Tone's friend Thomas Russell. It is perhaps significant that its library was tucked away in a corner of the Linen Hall, for along with Presbyterian clergymen intelligent businessmen were the mainstay of these societies. In 1812 the citizens of Belfast, led by William Drennan who, after a rather disappointing career in radical politics, had come back to Belfast, crowned their voluntary educational efforts by founding the Academical Institution, a school with a sort of college appendix, which it was thought might develop into a northern university. In fact it did form part of the foundation of the later Queen's College. This earnest belief in education sprang largely from the fact that over a third of the town's population—and a very influential third—was presbyterian. The Presbyterians had a traditional respect for learning, close academic contacts with Scotland, and a taste for theological dialetics which found full scope in the great debate over subscription which raged all over Ulster during the early nineteenth century. This did not, however, absorb by any means all their critical pugnacity for they had plenty left for politics. At the close of the eighteenth century, Belfast had been a focus of Irish radicalism. Its energetic non-conformist businessmen had been delighted by the victories of the rebels in America and of the Third Estate in France. The Society of United Irishmen had been founded in the town, and the *Northern Star,* published by a group of Belfast businessmen, had been the most lively and outspoken radical newspaper in Ireland. This radicalism in spite of the losses suffered in 1798, continued into the nineteenth century. Admittedly, the citizens of Belfast could not exercise any direct political power, for the Corporation of Belfast which returned a member to the Imperial parliament and was responsible for managing the town, was composed of persons who held their places for life and who were co-opted on the nomination of the Marquess of Donegall, the great local magnate. Owing to the Corporation's lethargy, the citizens, before 1841, were performing through other elected bodies many of the normal functions of local government. One of these bodies, the Governors of the Charitable Society incidentally managed to combine charity and enterprise in a remarkable way. They took over the management of the town's water supply which they greatly improved, and on which they made a profit devoted partly to building a new house of industry. Then to keep the inmates busy they started cotton spinning and this introduced a new industry into Belfast.

On general political issues public opinion in Belfast during the early nineteenth century was vocal and radical. In one important respect however the radicalism of the north of Ireland slowly but perceptibly changed. Nationalism ceased to be one of its essential elements.

This is easily explained. Irish nationalism from the beginning of the nineteenth century was politically speaking a protest against the union. But the union had inaugurated a period of great and growing prosperity for the north east of Ulster. Moreover, the great majority of inhabitants of Belfast shared the cultural and intellectual interests of Great Britain. Therefore, it is not surprising that their radicalism became almost undistinguishable from British liberalism. This change can be illustrated in several ways. For instance during the early years of the century Drennan, after his return to Belfast, edited for a while the *Belfast Magazine;* and a little later Lawless, a flamboyant journalist and unceasing but unselfish egoist, ran the *Irishman,* a newspaper. Both these ventures strongly emphasised the importance of preserving Irish nationalism. Both after a time collapsed. On the other hand, the *Northern Whig,* founded in 1826, which combined sturdy radicalism with an unswerving support of the union, flourished. Again, after the Reform victory, in Belfast as across the channel, a large section of the newly enfranchised middle class passed over to the conservative camp and the liberal intellectuals of the older school lost their grip on the town's politics.

If comparisons are odious, contrasts are often obvious. So in conclusion, I feel it is enough to say that Dublin and Belfast, by 1850 the largest cities in Ireland, were extraordinarily different. Dublin had the variety and dignity of a historical capital, together with something of the despair and decay of a dethroned capital, and the tensions and complexities of a city in which an old ascendancy was slowly relinquishing its place to a new democracy discontented with the general political situation. Belfast, on the other hand, was essentially a successful nineteenth century city, a tremendous concentration of creative industrial force in confident harmony with the main tendencies of the age.

BROADSTONE STATION, DUBLIN

II

THE COUNTRY HOUSE —
THE LIFE OF THE
GENTRY

BY HUBERT BUTLER

I WONDER IF a century ever closed with such drama and finality as marked the passing of eighteenth century Ireland. New men, new measures, new ideas at once came on the scene and those who had spent themselves in the tragedy and intellectual turmoil that preceded the Union all at once became antiquated figures, left high and dry in a world that had little use for them. Perhaps it was in the country houses that the spirit of the eighteenth century lingered longest. One thinks of Edgeworthstown House, the most illustrious of them all, and a carriage making its way across the bog to Castlepollard, one February day in 1817. In it sits an elderly much-muffled invalid, R. L. Edgeworth, and beside him his daughter Maria. They are on their way to visit Lord Longford's new bride, and Maria is reading him the first chapter of her novel *Ormond*. She is working against time for she knows that her father has not long to live and she is anxious that as he has shared in the writing of this book, he should at least see it in proof. And he too with his wide ranging eighteenth century mind is conscious of many other obligations to fulfil before he dies. There is a new bridge to be built and Mr. Fallon, the contractor, to be seen at Longford; there is a scheme to be prepared for an interdenominational elementary school in Edgeworthstown, which he hopes that his son, Lovel, will carry into effect upon his death. And he is wondering how Maria will get on without him. He must fortify her against the importunities of her younger brothers and sisters. She is business-like and will be rich but she is generous to a fault, and though he is proud of this gifted brood, which does such credit to himself and their elder sister, Maria, all the same there are complications in their characters . . . There is Francis for example . . .

One has the fancy that as they jog along they are leaving a full century behind them and plunging deeper and deeper into an empty one. Of course that is a ridiculous way to refer to the century of the steam engine, of electoral reform and Queen Victoria, but it is terribly true for the Irish country gentleman. Old Mr. Edgeworth's mind was as tightly packed with notions as Sir Jonah Barrington's with memories or as Lady Blessington's ballroom with gay and distinguished guests. He had no conception of the vacuities that yawned ahead.

For it was not only from politics that the next generations were to feel themselves excluded. From every field the gifted country gentleman was to find himself evicted by the specialist and the civil servant. His most formidable enemies were not, I think, a resentful tenantry, but the salaried professional who came to adorn the chairs and institutes which often owed their existence to the schemes hatched by the library fire, the lonely experiments in the outhouse or the observatory in the garden. Frankenstein had come to grips with his monster. I was told that when some years ago Edgeworthstown House was up for auction, strange mechanical contraptions were found in the loft. We are so apt now to smile at these lonely fancies from the provinces that it is not easy to visualise a world in which old Mr. Edgeworth could have been called by the government from his County Longford library to organise a telegraph from Dublin to Galway so that Dublin should have news of a French invasion. He spent two years at it and manned it with a telegraph corps from his yeomanry and tenants and he refused all financial reward. A couple of years later he served as a commissioner for the Board of Education in Ireland and the government of Revolutionary France appealed for his advice about industrial development. In the meantime he was reflecting on the construction of carriages and the making of roads, to such purpose that his biographer says that the tarred MacAdam of our century should rightfully be called tarred Edgeworth. As a member of parliament, he had spoken logically and forcibly against the Union. He was also collaborating with Maria in the writing of treatises on education and as we have seen contributing whole chapters to her famous novels.

But my illustration would be pointless if Edgeworth had been a man of sublime genius capable of overriding all obstacles. He was merely a landlord with an experimental turn of mind, wide interests and a good education, and to such a man the eighteenth century was kindly. A remote estate and a large family were not handicaps to the gratification of ambition.

There were many other survivors besides Edgeworth but the eighteen twenties saw most of them in their graves. You will see how abruptly provincial life fizzled out if you are lucky enough to find an old country house library whose shelves have not been combed by the dealer. You will certainly find the wide bottom shelf still occupied by the vast handsomely bound volumes of the proceedings of the Irish House of Commons, because no dealer is interested in these. They are too bulky for anything but pulping, though I have seen them used effectively as door stoppers. And above them there are probably rows of angry leather-bound pamphlets. Take one down and you will find some furious diatribe about jobbery or Arian heresies or a local election. There are equally fiery poems with significant blanks conveying to the well-informed the most appalling innuendoes. It is all very intimate and local, one of the neighbours is called Brutus and the other Beelzebub or Judas but as you cannot now guess what nobleman or country squire is hidden under this antique dress, you put the book back on the shelf. It is as mysterious as the roar of the ocean heard in an empty cockle shell. How is it possible that the ancestors of one's kind sensible neighbours were once so inflamed and eloquent?

But as you work your way round the library you will see how the change came about. Soon after the Union the pamphlets thinned out. Judas and Beelzebub had crossed to Westminster and somehow the shafts of Irish satire are only really deadly at very close range. About the 1820's the philosophy and the plays end and the sermons begin, with here and there, like an island, Walter Scott or a geological survey. And then even the sermons dry up and a very waste period begins and sometimes it never ends.

No doubt I am generalising far too much, but in some way we've got to account for that appalling smugness which creeps over the Irish gentry, like a paralysis, as the century advanced. At first it had quite a genial aspect, there was less abuse, less violence, less drink, less extravagance. I think it was merely that the Rakes of Mallow had taken their money and their merriment to Bath and Brighton! A great crop of charitable institutions and alms houses grew up, there were bible

28

classes and farming classes. In the drawingrooms where chair covers had been embroidered to the sound of the harpsichord, acres upon acres of warm cross-over shawls were knitted, in the kitchens where rum punch had been brewed, gallons of soup and mountains of nourishing jellies were prepared for the deserving poor. It is said that Lady Elizabeth Fownes literally killed herself with woolwork; and at Piltown the four daughters of Lord Duncannon regularly taught in the village school. Hand in hand with this there was a religious revival among the Protestant gentry. How was it that these improved manners did not lead to friendlier feelings but instead the old bitterness intensified, the old divisions deepened?

I think that the answer is that the upper classes had been scared first by the French revolution and then by the '98 rebellion. In the memoirs of Dorothea Herbert, the Tipperary clergyman's daughter, you get a wonderful picture of that wave of horror and repudiation that swept across Ireland, assisted no doubt by Castlereagh and Fitzgibbon and their kind but based also on vivid personal experiences. Dorothea's opinions were ordinary, she is only extravagant in the freedom with which she expresses herself. She gives incidentally a vivid picture of the uninhibited gaiety and gorgeousness of the Irish provinces, before the thunderbolt had fallen. Do you remember her account of the Cashel races, their new bottle-green silver-plated coach and the glass vis-a-vis of their cousin Ned Eyre and how he attended the Assembly Ball that night in "a pink lutestring suit blazing with brilliants from top to toe, and covered with double paste buttons on cuffs, knees and shoes"? The dominant theme through the memoirs is of course her unrequited love for John Roe of Rockwell, but I don't think that, without the horrors of the rebellion, the anguish of the heart alone would have unhinged her reason. While they were away from Knockgrafton rectory her nurse had been riddled with bullets by the rebels and the sexton had been hacked to pieces with a chopper.

Such things had happened all over Ireland and only a handful could risk being dispassionate and try to analyse the origins of cruelty, the nemesis of injustice. Dorothea Herbert seeing the bloodstains on the rectory carpet plunged deeper into a region of horror and hallucination from which she seems never to have returned. At the end of her memoirs it is plain that she has gone out of her mind. Though revulsion seldom took such extreme forms, the bulk of the Irish gentry did, after the rebellion, plunge into a mood of stern self-righteousness, and moral repudiation of lawlessness. One cannot call it hyprocritical, because hardly anyone of any party or faith defended the rebellion, except those implicated in it. In Cruikshank's illustrations to Maxwell's *History of the Rebellion,* you see this mood of self-satisfaction at its most repulsive—small girls transfixed with pikes at the barn of Scullabogue, drunken peasants dancing jigs on grand pianos, while their blowsy wives with a bottle to their lips tear the portraits from their frames and trample on the Holy Bible.

Every respectable person was thinking along those lines, and it needed courage and independence of mind in a high degree to swim upstream against so strong a current. Naturally the British did not want to see too much cordiality between the two Irish parties. They had been scared by the rapprochement that had led to the volunteer movement and to Grattan's Parliament. So everything was done to play on the fears of the Anglo-Irish.

Because of all this there was a revulsion not only

against the idealism of Grattan's volunteers but also against the easy lavish ways, the liberal speculation, the generous acknowledgment of the right to think otherwise, which had been characteristic of the movement. The educated 18th century gentleman was not averse to experiment in politics, religion, morals; I don't mean that he was more irreligious or immoral than his forebears or descendants but to a surprising degree he was uninfluenced by those two solemn considerations that weighed so heavily on a later age; "What will the neighbours think?" and "What would happen if my tenants got hold of these ideas?".

It appeared to the post union gentry that "ideas" had much to answer for, and they began to criticize their humanist ancestors for tolerating them and even publishing books about them. "Ideas!" that was what led to the guillotine and to Wolfe Tone, to the calamity that had fallen on the respectable Emmets, the disgrace of the noble Fitzgeralds. Down with ideas.

The result was that one has the impression of a whole generation tip-toeing round their subordinates, ready to make any concession, except the perilous liberty of independent thinking. When they erected a pillar in Sackville Street it was not Grattan they put on top of it, but Nelson, who had safeguarded Britain from the pernicious doctrines of Revolutionary France, a Nelson who was made the pattern of chivalry and whose eighteenth century morals were tactfully ignored. And as for the Duke of Wellington, an Irishman married to an Irishwoman, even Maria Edgeworth lost her head about him, monuments sprang up to him right and left and little local societies all over Ireland wrote to him asking him to be their patron. But the Duke had his feet firmly planted in the logical eighteenth century and refused all these invitations with notes which would have been offensive if they had not been personal and painstaking. "The Duke of Wellington," he replied to one such invitation, "fails to see the value of joining a society, whose meetings he would be unable to attend."

The Duke, in this way, unconsciously perhaps, challenged the delusion of the nineteenth century Irishman, that he could spread his wings in the wide imperial world, which the British laid open to him, and not lose his foothold in the small community in which he was reared but whose meetings "he would be unable to attend". In fact the story of the wealthy talented Wellesleys illustrates accurately what was happening all over Ireland to the indigenous gentry. When Mrs. Delany, a generation earlier, had visited the family in their splendid mansion, Dangan, near Trim, the head of the house was still busy laying out artificial lakes and planting trees. They still called themselves Wesley in those days but the name was getting middle-class revivalist associations and they were anxious to be rid of it. Mr. Wesley was a cultivated gentleman, who turned to the classics for entertainment. He used to give all his guests white walking sticks engraved with the names of classical deities, whom they might be supposed to resemble and they went for stately walks in keeping with the characters they represented. The Wesleys were all very gifted, some played a part in Dublin musical societies, others in Co. Meath. They seemed perfectly established there and yet already the tide was flowing away from Ireland. It was inevitable that little Arthur's talents, displayed in those days in making miniature fortresses on the lake, should draw him away to England and that his brother should look for fame in India. Remarkably soon Dangan had been sold to a speculator. He insured it heavily and, most opportunely, it immediately took fire. You pass the ruins to-day

EMO HOUSE, THE SEAT OF THE EARL OF PORTARLINGTON

between Trim and Athboy. They stand in the remnants of a park and no one could guess that they commemorate a catastrophe a century earlier than the neighbouring Georgian ruins of the nineteen twenties, Summerhill and the others. There was no particular tragedy about the burning of Dangan. The house was only a stage in the passage of imperial glory; but obviously these voluntary departures weakened the confidence of those who remained. After the Union many of the enterprising and intelligent began to speak with the lukewarm conviction of temporary lodgers. They were not prepared to commit themselves as deeply as their ancestors had done.

But of course there were exceptions to all this. There was a small group of the Irish gentry living in the neighbourhood of Thomastown, who felt that they still had something to offer to Ireland exclusively and who did not intend to abdicate their responsibilities or be thrust aside. The best known of them was Charles Kendal Bushe, the Incorruptible, who had made the celebrated speech against the Union. The prologues of the Kilkenny Players have been quoted once or twice already on Radio Eireann, but one of them is so appropriate that I will risk repeating it. It is a forlorn appeal to the Irish gentry to stay in Ireland where their roots were and not follow the tide of fashion to England where they would only be patronised as remote provincials. It is written by one of Bushe's sons.

> The worthy Esquire sells his old estate
> Possessed with proud ambition to be great
> And what's his view of greatness? to be sent
> An independent man to Parliament.
> And truly independent, forth he goes,
> of all the comforts his old home bestows.

See him in London to a chop house sneak
To famish on a solitary steak.
Yet on each meal more substance wasting
Than here would furnish hospitable feasting.
Or see him round St. James' purlieus straying
with wonderous eyes that wealthy world surveying
and half his income for a garret paying.
Or at St. Stephen's on a top bench waiting
in fretful doze while statesmen are debating,
unknown, unnoticed save by some pert peer,
who thus accosts his neighbour with a sneer,
'Who's that, my Lord? His face I don't remember'.
'How could you? 'Tis a Scotch or Irish member.
They come and go in droves but we don't know
     'em.
They should have keepers, like wild beasts, to
     show 'em.
But wait a moment till he gives his vote,
and then you'll know his nation by his note'.

The Kilkenny Theatre season scarcely lasted twenty
years, yet it became a rallying point for all those in
whom the critical, conciliatory, gay and sceptical
eighteenth century spirit survived. It is sad that the
most embittered opposition which it met came from
the ardent but very narrow reforming element in the
Protestant Church to which I have already referred.
The Rev. Peter Roe of St. Mary's denounced the theatre
as 'a gilded bait to lure souls into Satan's net' and with
execration he recorded the precise number of rectors,
canons, deans, archdeacons and even bishops, who had
abandoned themselves to these biennial orgies of
Sheridan and Shakespeare.

I can think of many philantrophic enterprises of this
time but over most of them there broods the panic fear

of democracy, of liberalism. Class distinctions were registered in Heaven but it was right to alleviate the sufferings of the poor. When Lovel Edgeworth started the schools at Edgeworthstown, which his father had planned, he decreed that during school hours linen smocks were to be worn to conceal the distinctions of rank which the boy's rags or fine clothes might betray. But after school there was to be no mixing, 'to avoid,' said Lovel, 'the alarming appearance of a democratic tendency'. Then there were a few ventures like the Merino cloth factory at Annamult on the Nore, an experiment in economic and social organisation such as R. L. Edgeworth would have approved of. Some progressive local gentry sank and lost a good deal of money in it and for ten or fifteen years the fields were white with vast woolly sheep from Spain and the looms were busy; a village was built and a church for the workers whose needs and hopes were carefully studied. They said of it in a Kilkenny Prologue:

'There sports and toil the alternate hours beguile

And man, poor labouring man is taught to smile.'
But on the whole very little was done to realise that dream of unity, which had been an inspiration to Grattan and his colleagues.

Elizabeth Bowen in her book *Bowen's Court* says of this period that, after the Union 'from the big lord to the small country gentleman, they were being edged back upon a tract of clouds and obsessions . . . the sense of dislocation was everywhere. Property was still there but power was going'. And she tells a story of Lord Kingston which is so illuminating that I will repeat it. He was the landlord of Mitchelstown, wealthy, farseeing, magnificent, the very type of benevolent despot. When his despotism was threatened, not only did his benevolence disappear but even his reason.

He went mad. This is how it happened. He was, I ought to have said, the creator of the broad streets of Mitchelstown, the pleasant college square, a Protestant and a Catholic Church. His estates were models of humane and efficient management. But he loathed industrialism and when he saw a tall chimney go up in Mitchelstown he took a solemn farewell to the townsfolk and told them with a breaking voice that he was leaving for England the next day for there was no room in Mitchelstown for himself and the owner of the chimney. That evening the manufacturer was obliged to receive some uninvited guests and a couple of days later he had gone.

It was democracy as much as Ireland that finished Lord Kingston or Big George as he was called. Soon after this episode there was a by-election in Limerick and Big George, confident that his tenantry would vote as he told them, organised them into a mile long procession to the city. When he learnt a little later that to a man they had voted against his candidate the bottom fell out of his world. For a paternal despot it was an insult beyond forgiveness. He summoned all the tenantry of three counties to the long gallery in Mitchelstown Castle. For a few moments he gazed at them in speechless stupefaction and then suddenly . . . he went mad. Jumping from his chair, he screamed, 'They are come to tear me to pieces!' A little later he was removed struggling by his servants and that was the end of Big George's duel with democracy.

I doubt whether the era of aristocratic rule ended so dramatically in other countries. But the defeat of the Beresford candidate in Waterford, through the interposition of Daniel O'Connell was a sensation of even greater magnitude. The Irish landlords of the ascendancy had loathed Wolfe Tone, but he spoke a language which they understood and abhorred, as later, in the same way, they were to loathe Parnell. Yet I think their real detestation was for Daniel O'Connell, whose powerful influence was outside their comprehension. There were qualities in him which should have warmed their hearts, if narrow self-interest alone had been consulted, his hatred of revolution, his loyalty to the young queen, his indifference to Irish culture. But I believe it was from their contact with O'Connell and the deep mass-emotion which he organised against them, that they first began to feel themselves irremediably alien. And they minded far more being called alien than being called blood-suckers or parasites. For it appears that landlordism, good or bad, is an inevitable stage in social development. Daniel O'Connell was a landlord, evicting his tenants like everybody else. Smith O'Brien was a landlord and led his tenants to challenge the British Government at the battle of the Cabbage Patch. It is a phenomenon which would run its appointed course, whatever the source of authority. But to be called an alien is far more bruising since you cannot change your blood and I think that in the early nineteenth century, many of the gentry despairing of politics were trying to restore in the field of letters and science and scholarship that idea of a united people, which Castlereagh had once quenched and which O'Connell was unlikely to favour. I am not thinking of the followers of Thomas Davis, whose motives were avowedly political, but of less sanguine people who decided to study the country which they could not rule.

Perhaps the times being what they were, they had chosen well, because there is scarcely any course of study relating to Ireland which you can pursue very far without running into the work of some early nine-teenth century scholar from a Big House, who has managed to prove he was Irish by being indispensable to Ireland. It is mostly conscientious, unostentatious work, often defiantly parochial and as unexciting to the general public as it was unremunerative to its author. That fine series of county surveys, organised by the R.D.S., was never better done than when entrusted to a local squire like William Tighe. County histories began to be written and county archaeological societies founded. If you look at the membership lists of these old societies you will see how fully they justified their claims to be impartial and representative and how often in their hands history, contrary to her usual habit, seemed, when investigated without prejudice, to heal old grievances rather than to inflame them. In the second quarter of the nineteenth century all Ireland was traversed by scholars in gigs and dog carts measuring raths, recording legends, evolving theories or even more enthusiastically refuting them. It was the age of Graves and Prim as well as of O'Donovan and O'Curry and in almost every Irish country house you will find traces of its passage; perhaps it is some feeble antiquarian water colour on the wall; perhaps it is a pile of dusty archaeological journals in the attic.

And if you look at the minute-books of these old societies you will be astonished at the venom and the vigour with which ignorant officials and barbarian landowners are chastised. It is as though, like their grandfathers, these country scholars saw their opponents in the guise of Judas or Beelzebub. But we owe a great deal to their ill-temper. If it had not been for these unofficial bodies with their backbone of educated country gentleman, Newgrange would have been destroyed to make a county Meath by-road and Clonmacnois and Glendalough would have been irreparably damaged.

I dare say, through concentrating on political frustration and its antidotes, I have given a too morbid and melancholy picture of this period. I think that even in Ireland only two per-cent of the human race ever worries for long about political frustration and I should have told you more about hunting and sport and travel and gardening. But I could not have done that without also speaking of the sons and daughters, who worked outside Ireland and whose visits and adventures filled the house with reflected glory and excitement. Undoubtedly Irish country houses often had and still have this kind of glamour. But I have been thinking of them as places which once generated light and diffused it. I have been voicing the discontent of the restless two per cent. Their views are not, of course, very representative but to balance that you must remember they are very seldom heard.

III

RURAL LIFE

BY T. P. O'NEILL

MANY CHANGES HAVE occurred in Irish rural life in the last hundred years or so. The great catastrophe of the famine just over a hundred years ago initiated a stream of emigration which halved the population. The effects of the crisis were seen in new social relationships and a redistribution of wealth. This was helped by the reforms of the land laws in the second half of the nineteenth century which abolished landlordism and made farmers into landowners instead of tenants. The social change was all the greater because of the developments in mechanisation and the impact of industrialism and mass production which replaced many distinctive domestic utensils and farm tools, made by local craftsmen, by factory wares.

In every district in Ireland objects are to be found which call to mind the mode of life of our ancestors. Rushlight candlesticks and wooden vessels, which years ago were part of the equipment of the homes of the people, are quite common and recall a more primitive scene than that which is to be found to-day. The findings of objects of domestic use or obsolete farm implements may conjure up a picture of an era of hard work and little luxury but it can scarcely bring to mind the full extent of the misery and poverty in which the bulk of the population of rural Ireland lived in the decades before the great famine of 1846 and the following years.

Occasionally a farmer unearths a hearthstone in what
is now an open field or even a few hearths in an area
where no memory survives of any family having lived.
These are the few solid remains of mud cabins which
were found throughout the countryside and whose
occupants have died of fever or hunger or been
scattered to the ends of the earth.

The grim scene which a traveller encountered in
Ireland at that time can be gathered from the description
given by Gustave de Beaumont, a Frenchman who
visited this country in the 1830's:

> "To see Ireland happy you must carefully select
> your point of view, look for some narrow, isolated
> spot, and shut your eyes to all the objects that
> surround it; but wretched Ireland, on the contrary
> bursts upon your view everywhere.
>
> "Misery, naked and famishing, that misery which
> is vagrant, idle, and mendicant covers the entire
> country; it shows itself everywhere, and at every
> hour of the day; it is the first thing you see when
> you land on the Irish coast, and from that moment
> it ceases not to be present to your view."

The various strata of society in rural Ireland of just
over a century ago may be judged on the strength of
the hold which each class had on land. Land was the
sole intervening bulwark between the Irish rural family
and starvation. First of all there was the farmer with
a reasonably firm hold on his land provided he paid
his rent. Of course he had not the security in most cases
of a lease and was never sure that his rent would not be
raised by his landlord but at least he had a piece of land
however small and had the social status of a farmer.
These farmers varied in prosperity according to the
size and quality of their holdings but by far the greater

number held very small farms. More than four out of every five farmers held less than fifteen acres of land. Almost one half of the farmers held less than five acres. The standard of living of those with small holdings was very similar to that of the agricultural labourer. They frequently sold the produce of all their land, except the acre of potato ground, to pay their rent, and lived on the produce of the potato plot.

The agricultural labourer usually had a plot of ground attached to his cabin and that he cultivated to produce potatoes for his family. He paid the rent in labour and received no money wages as they were cancelled against his rent. Occasionally he might draw an advance of a shilling or two for necessities of life— "Cash for a coat, 5/9." "Cash for the Priest 1/0." "Cash to go to the races 1/0." These were kept in an account book by the employer and totalled with the rent. Sometimes tally sticks were notched to make accounts of days worked by the labourer. In November and April the accounts were balanced and the labourer could have a few shillings due to him or he could owe his employer some money. The pig was the main means by which the labourer paid off any debts over and above those which his labour had paid. The agricultural labourer renting his cabin and garden from a large farmer was assured of constant employment—sufficient at least to meet his rent. Thus he had a certain amount of security.

His neighbour who had but a cabin and no fixed plot of ground lived a much more precarious existence. He had no constant employment and tried to live by taking land by conacre. The rents charged were high particularly for manured ground—usually about £10 an Irish acre. The person taking conacre secured a certain amount of profitable employment and guaranteed a supply of food for his family. However, he gambled on the crops. If they failed he was not in a position to pay his rent. Part of the rent he paid in cash and part in labour. Conacre was the least secure of the footholds on subsistence which an Irish family could have had and it was, in fact, a step towards being completely cut off from land.

Labourers started work at 6 a.m. and were paid at rates ranging from 4*d*. to 8*d*. a day with diet or 8*d*. to a shilling a day without diet. These payments were largely nominal and were mainly cancelled against rents. Rates of wages were slightly higher in summer than in winter and in spring and harvest the labourer. wives and children earned a few shillings at sowing or picking potatoes or binding corn. Normally, however, work was scarce and there was little constant employment. It was calculated in 1836 that the average employment covered only a total of twenty-two weeks in the year. In some parts of the country the position was worse than in others. The result was that labourers moved from one district to another seeking work. From Cork they went into Limerick and Tipperary and from the West of Ireland they went across the midlands. Throughout the years before the famine large numbers of labourers went to Scotland and England for harvest work. On these trips they saved some money to pay the rent of their little plots of potato ground. In their absence their families frequently lived by begging especially during the "hungry months" or "meal months" of June and July after the year's stock of potatoes had been used up and before the new ones became available. The cabins of both the farmers and labourers were very much alike. The French traveller I have already quoted described one in the following terms:

"Imagine four walls of dried mud, (which the rain, as it falls, easily restores to its primitive condition) having for its roof a little straw or some sods, for its chimney a hole cut in the roof, or very frequently the door through which alone the smoke finds an issue. One single apartment contains father, mother, children and sometimes a grandfather or a grandmother; there is no furniture in this wretched hovel; a single bed of straw serves the entire family. Five or six half-naked children maye be seen crouched near a miserable fire, the ashes of which cover a few potatoes, the sole nourishment of the family. In the midst of all lies a dirty pig, the only thriving inhabitant of the place, for he lives in filth. The presence of the pig in an Irish hovel may at first seem an indication of misery; on the contrary, it is a sign of comparative comfort. Indigence is still more extreme in the hovel where no pig is to be found . . .

"This dwelling is very miserable, still it is not that of the pauper properly so called. I have just described the dwelling of the Irish farmer or agricultural labourer."

The cabins were usually about twelve feet broad and ranged in length from twelve to twenty-one feet. The smaller ones consisted of only one room which served as a kitchen living room and bedroom. Almost one half of the families in Ireland in 1841 lived in one roomed cabins. The walls of the cabins were made of mud, occasionally on a foundation of stone. There were in many instances no windows, or the places which originally held a pane of glass were filled with straw or old rags or even completely closed with mud. The only ironwork in the cabins was the hooks from which the doors hung. The doors themselves were frequently made of wickerwork and sometimes even a piece of furze served the purpose of a door. Shutters and bolts were unknown in many districts. The chimneys, where they existed at all, consisted of wickerwork and mud. Those which had no chimneys had sometimes a hole in the thatch or in the end wall to allow the smoke to escape though often its only exit was the doorway.

The floor was the natural earth and was sunken one or even two feet under the level of the ground outside the walls. It was usually uneven and holes in it were used to feed the pig. The sunken floor suffered greatly from damp because of its low level and of the roof not being rainproof. In bogs cabins were sometimes built against banks and others were made by raising dwarf walls around pits dug three or four feet below the surface of the bog so that the cabins were half above and half below the ground. A sub-inspector of police in Kells barony in County Meath stated in 1836 that he and his patrol on one occasion "came to what appeared to be a roughly thatched roof of a cabin but even with the surface of the bog where it was situated; upon examination they found it to be really a human habitation, occupied by a labourer and his family. It was formed of an old turf excavation, six or seven feet deep, over which a roof had merely been put to form a house." The only means of getting in or out was by a ladder of sticks in one corner.

The roofing of cabins was made of sods of earth, laid on rafters. Oaten or wheaten straw was used for thatch, but it was usually very decayed and was sometimes replaced by rushes and even potato stalks. The rafters were made of rough pieces of wood and were bent, broken and propped up in all directions. Rain seeped through at many points and bedding had to be moved from one place to another to avoid the leaks.

The furniture of the cabin was as primitive as the cabin itself. There was seldom a proper bed but usually a rough wooden structure raising the straw on which the family slept off the ground. A labourer in Galway described such a makeshift bed:

> "Two holes in the wall . . . answer instead of the two head bed-posts, . . . two forked sticks driven in the floor answer for the end bed-posts; resting on these are two stretchers or long sticks, and across these stretchers are laid wattles upon which the straw is spread."

A great number of families slept on the floor and even when there was a bed children had frequently to sleep on rushes on the floor. Bedclothes were practically non-existent. Most houses had but one blanket and frequently only half a blanket. All covered themselves at night with their day clothes. When there was but one room the families slept together though in some places boys slept behind a screen of mats. They tended to huddle together for warmth which their ragged clothes did not give.

The other furniture consisted of three or four three-legged stools in place of chairs, a wooden chest, sometimes a table (but most families placed a potato basket on a pot to serve as a table), a can for carrying water, a knife, a pewter or iron spoon, two or three plates, either of delph or wood, and an iron pot. Some had small dressers of two or three shelves but usually the shelves were built into a recess in a wall.

Clothing in general was very bad. In the early years of the century frieze was made by the labourers and farmers themselves in their own homes but gradually this was replaced by inferior qualities of cloth which were cheaper to buy than the cost of making their former type. It was unusual for a labourer to have an overcoat. His apparel consisted of a shirt, waistcoat, trousers, boots, stockings, and a frieze body coat. These, however, were worn to a thread and patched and re-patched until they became practically unrecognisable. Women's clothes consisted of a cloak, dress, petticoat, shift, cap and apron. Women seldom wore shoes though the wives of small farmers generally had one pair which they wore when going to Mass or to fairs and markets. They always carried them in their hands, however, until they came near the town or church and then put them on. The cheap manufactured cottons helped to improve the appearance of the women's clothes but they were frequently insufficiently clad and lacked warm under-clothes. Much of the clothing was bought secondhand at fairs and markets or from pawnbrokers and quite an amount of it appears to have been brought over to Ireland from dealers in London and Liverpool.

The clothing of the old and the young was even worse. The cast off, or fallen-off, clothing of the father passed on to the children who from the age of ten months to ten years were practically naked. They had but rags tied or stitched together which barely served the purposes of decency and imparted little or no protection against cold. The children practically always went barefoot.

The food of the bulk of Irish rural families was potatoes. There was, apparently, a deterioration in this respect in the decades after the end of the Napoleonic Wars. The better quality potatoes were known as "cups" and "apples" but the poor had little chance of eating them. Instead they were forced to eat inferior quality known as "lumpers". They were more prolific than the better varieties but were coarser. It was generally accepted that the poor should eat only the "lumper". On one occasion when a landlord saw the daughter of one of his tenants washing potatoes at the door of a cabin, he noticed that they were of the apple kind and asked her were they for the dinner. Upon being answered that they were he entered the house and asked for an explanation why the tenant dared eat apple potatoes, which fetched a good price in Dublin, while in debt for rent. It was considered a treat for a labourer to have buttermilk with potatoes and even those who owned a horse and a cow could not afford to eat butter or eggs. They had to sell them to make up the rent. They usually had salt as a condiment but little else to lend flavour. Occasionally, near the seacoast, a few herrings were bought but practically never flesh meat except at Christmas and Easter.

There were normally three meals a day, all of potatoes, but in scarce months of summer, labourers had to confine themselves to two or even one meal a day. In May, June and July they were sometimes obliged to eat nettles and a weed called "praiseach" or charlock. Occasionally whole families fasted for more than twenty-four hours. During bad seasons, when potato crops failed, whole families were destitute and famine and starvation were rife. During these periods the poor lived on charity or got into debt to dealers who sold potatoes from other parts of Ireland at exorbitant profits. The use of oatmeal or wheaten flour was practically unknown, except to the more comfortable farmers who were able to turn to them during the months before new potatoes were available. For weddings or such festivities it was considered a delicacy to have wheaten bread.

Tobacco was smoked by most labourers and was

SKIBBEREEN

probably their only luxury. Those attending weddings and wakes drank a great deal of whiskey. The poverty of the people prevented excessive drinking except on rare occasions. Fuel was mainly turf cut from a bank rented from the landlord. This was frequently inadequate and was supplemented by the children collecting dried cow and horse manure, weeds, and bits of sticks from hedges. In areas where there were no turf bogs the poor suffered severely from scarcity of fuel and it was frequently found, during severe winters, that the provision of fuel for the poor was more essential than food. Candles were not bought, except at Christmas. Instead rushes dipped in grease, hemp dipped in resin or bog deal were used to provide light. Soap was little used, rainwater being used instead.

The periods when there was little employment were spent by the men in going around from house to house chatting and discussing the news. A great number of feast days were observed as holidays and were occasions for testing feats of strength and prowess at games. The most dangerous problem in many Irish parishes was the existence of factions between whom cudgel fights flared up with little provocation at patterns and fairs. The faction fights were common in all parts of the country until the 1830's when the Under Secretary, Thomas Drummond, succeeded in putting an end to them. Race meetings were occasions of great festivities as were weddings and wakes. Many of the stories of William Carleton depict scenes of gaiety and joy in the midst of poverty for despite the hardship of his lot the Irishman appears to have been able to forget his cares.

When men gathered together they tried their strength at long-jumping, lifting weights and throwing the sledge. In some parts of the country a game called bowls, which still survives in Cork, was played. In Armagh it was known as bullets. Football was also played but the main game was hurling. The rules of these games were not laid down in an exact code but certain rules were accepted. Wrestling among the players was admissible and the games were tests of endurance and skill.

Throughout the early nineteenth century the condition of the Irish people gave rise to much comment and was the subject of many parliamentary enquiries. The government in Westminster did nothing to alleviate the position. There were partial famines in 1822, 1831, 1835, 1836 and 1837, 1839 and 1842—all warnings of the danger to the population should the potato crop fail. The only remedial measure introduced was the provision of a poor law system under which the poor could be maintained in workhouses. These grim buildings were erected in all parts of Ireland between 1838 and 1843. They were operated in such a manner that they would attract only those in danger of starving. All liberty was lost within their walls and they were practically gaols.

This poor law did nothing to get at the root of the evil in Ireland. It provided a means of alleviating extreme poverty in normal years but it was not geared to cope with any major catastrophe. There was a physical limit to the number of persons any workhouse could hold and there was also a limit to the possible income from any rate levied locally to sustain the poor. The problems of high rents, insecurity of land tenure, undue competition for land were unchecked. Holdings continued to be sub-divided and the population continued to increase. There was no industrial development, except around Belfast, to absorb the growing population and to provide employment.

The problem was great and there was no easy means of solving it. Much could have been done at an earlier stage to prevent the situation becoming so desperate but once it had arisen the machinery of government was scarcely capable of dealing with it. There was a grave lack of capital among landowners and many of them lived abroad and did nothing for their tenants except draw their rents. The result was that undeveloped land was lying waste except where pressure of population forced cottiers to till land higher up the hills and deeper into bogs. There was no system of arterial drainage which would have helped to improve the waste lands. Governments, at that time too, were very reluctant to to interfere with the rights of property. The landlords themselves frequently had little money and even when willing to develop their estates they were impeded by lack of capital. An improving landlord could create even greater hardship than the one who took little interest in the management of his estate. The landlord who wished to improve his estate tried to remove the smallholders and consolidate the holdings into economic farms. The result was that families were thrown off the estate and became wholly destitute.

Observers throughout the first half of the nineteenth century pointed to the grave danger which existed of a total failure of the potato crop. One half of the Irish people had no other food and no means to purchase any other. Thus it was that when the new potato disease, the blight, made its appearance in the autumn of 1845 the country was filled with foreboding of a crisis. The crisis really came when the crop of 1846 was a total failure.

The condition of the people made the organisation of relief measures very difficult once the famine started. The poor were committed to paying rent to farmers for plots of potato ground which produced nothing but rotten potatoes. Their labour was already sold for rent and it created a social upheaval to take the labourers from the employers, who, in many places, were unable to pay money wages, and put them on public employment schemes. Another problem was that the rate of wages current before 1845 was somewhat nominal and the money earned was not sufficient to buy food for a family. It was barely enough to pay the rent of a potato plot. The wages on public works were, to some extent, tied to the local rates of pay but it was found that certain increases had to be allowed to enable the poor to buy alternative food. The lack of success which attended the schemes of relief stemmed largely from a lack of appreciation on the part of the officials of the intricacies of the Irish social background.

The overcrowding and insanitary condition of the cabins resulted in the spreading of fever when typhus made its appearance. Whole families were wiped out and far more died of fever during the famine than died of actual starvation. Hundreds of thousands fled from the stricken land. By the operation of a clause in the later relief measures, which excluded from assistance all who held more than a quarter acre of land, tenants were forced to surrender their holdings. Advantage was taken of the situation to consolidate farms and many of the smaller units disappeared. In 1841 there were over half a million farms of less than fifteen acres. Ten years later, just after the famine, this number had been reduced by half. Thus was practically eliminated the class which, before the famine, had the same standard of living as the labourer but the social status of a farmer. The famine had the effect of directing attention to the Irish question and solved the problem of the disparity between the population and production not by increasing the country's wealth but by drastically reducing the population. It commenced a movement which changed the face of rural Ireland and opened a new era in the economic, social and even political history of Ireland.

IV

EDUCATION AND THE PEOPLE

BY DAVID KENNEDY

IN MICHAEL MCLAVERTY'S short story, *The Game Cock,* one of the characters puts the following problem to a little boy: "A ropemaker made a rope for his marrying daughter, and in the rope he made twenty knots, and in each knot he put a purse, and in each purse he put seven threepenny bits and nine halfpennies. How much of a dowry did the daughter get?" When the boy fails to answer, his questioner upbraids him: "The scholars nowadays have soft brains. You can't do it with your pencil and paper, and an old man like me can do it in my head." To which the boy could only reply: "But we don't learn them kind of sums."

We have all been tortured in our youth by pedlars of similar arithmetical conundrums, and most of us have had to make the same reply. For "them kind of sums" come, not from the school texts of to-day but from those of the eighteenth century. You will find them in arithmetics of Dowling, Gough, Deighan and Voster. They belong to an age when arithmetic was a national pastime, and they passed from the schools into the homes of the people to become part of our folklore.

The three R's, reading, writing and arithmetic, are essential bread and butter subjects. The demand for them, and the manner in which the schools of Ireland satisfied it, at the beginning of the nineteenth century, reflect truly the economic background of the period.

Let me use a quotation from a novelist of the time, William Carleton, to sketch in the background. The speaker is a hedge-school master, and he addresses a poor scholar, Jemmy McEvoy, who is about to leave his native Ulster to seek learning in Munster, as Carleton himself did:

"Now, James, I'll tell you what you'll do when you reach the larned South. Plant yourself on the highest hill in the neighbourhood wherein the academician with whom you intend to stop lives. Let the hour of reconnoitring be that in which dinner is preparing. When seated there, James, take a survey of the smoke that ascends from the chimneys of the farmers' houses, and be sure to direct your steps to that from which the highest and merriest column rises. This is the old plan and it is a sure one. The highest smoke rises from the largest fire, the largest fire boils the biggest pot, the biggest pot holds the fattest bacon, and the fattest bacon is kept by the richest farmer. It is a wholesome and comfortable climax, my boy, and one by which I myself was enabled to keep a dacent portion of educated flesh between the master's birch and my ribs. The science itself is called Gastric Geography, and is peculiar to itinerant young gentlemen who seek for knowledge in the classical province of Munster."

The quotation gives the impression of a countryside at once prosperous and populous. Agricultural prices were soaring: the boom lasted at least until 1815. And even in the barren coastal lands there was remunerative employment to be found in the burning of kelp. Napoleon's blockade of England had produced this state of affairs which we have seen repeated in our time. Education was eagerly sought. The merchants' offices needed clerks and bookkeepers; the great estates needed surveyors and agriculturists; the multitude of small ships trading from Irish ports needed navigators. There was money available to give a lad of parts the schooling necessary for the church, or the law, or medicine. The demand for education was met, for the most part, by the growth of popular schools, the product of private enterprise, and entirely free from any form of State control or subsidy.

There did exist a comprehensive system of official schools. It had been initiated as part of the Tudor scheme of conquest. It covered primary, secondary and university education. The primary or parish schools owed their existence to an act of Henry VIII. The secondary or diocesan schools were established by Elizabeth I who founded the only Irish university, Trinity College, Dublin. To these the Stuarts added the Royal schools, endowed out of the plantation of Ulster. They were, like the diocesan schools, grammar schools where instruction in the grammar of the classics formed the core of the curriculum. But these schools touched only a small fraction of the population. In many places the statutory obligation to provide them, an obligation imposed on the established church, was ignored or evaded, and in some places the endowments were misappropriated. At the end of the eighteenth century a commission of inquiry reported that "they have not answered the intentions of the founders; that parish and diocesan schools, with very few exceptions, have been of little use to the public; and that the benefits from schools on Royal foundations have been totally inadequate to the expectations that might justly have been formed from their large endowments."

This awareness of the inefficiency of the official schools was not new. It had been recognised in the seventeenth century by the Cromwellian planter, Erasmus Smith, part of whose lands had been used to create a trust for the endowment of schools. The trust had been amended in 1723 to permit the founding of schools where more attention was to be paid to commercial and mathematical subjects than to the classics, and by 1800 some one hundred and fifty of these "English" schools, as they were called, had been built. It was recognised too, by the founders of the Incorporated Society for Promoting English Protestant Schools in Ireland. This was the body which conducted the notorious charter schools, and which was described by Dr. Drennan, the Ulster patriot, in a letter to the lord lieutenant in 1795 as "a charity which thrives on the extinction of all the other charities of life". Nevertheless the Society had been voted over one million pounds from public funds between 1745 and 1832. Then with the foundation of the National Board parliamentary aid was withdrawn from it and most of its schools disappeared.

Side by side with the ineffective and inefficient official system the people of Ireland maintained in the eighteenth and nineteenth centuries an unofficial—and indeed for a great time—an illegal system of schools. Perhaps it should not be called a system for it was not welded into a definite organisation. Schools developed where local needs demanded them, when and where a master was available. But in its heyday it was so widespread, so moulded by native genius as to have a national form, the same in Kerry as in Derry, that it might well be called a national system.

The schools were variously known as popular schools, pay schools and hedge schools. A hospitable farm-house might become a school for the winter months. In return for bread and board and accommodation for his scholars the master would give free tuition to his host's children. Often in summer, however, from choice as much as from necessity, the school would meet in the open air, sheltering from the sun or rain under a tree or hedge. Hence the name "hedge schools".

At the beginning of this talk I mentioned the utilitarian aspect of the curriculum in these schools. The protection given to Irish trade by the Irish parliament from 1782 to 1800 had stimulated the native schoolmasters to compile their own text-books on arithmetic. In them you will find, not only problems of the type I quoted expressed in language racy of the soil, but also more solid stuff "adapted to the trade and commerce of Ireland". Among these Gough of Lisburn, Dowling of Dublin and Voster of Cork had a nation-wide reputation. The proficiency of Irish lads in arithmetic was often commented on by outside observers. One quotation must suffice here: R. L. Edgeworth declared in 1808: "I am certain it will be found that not only the common but also the higher parts of arithmetic are better understood and more expertly practised by boys without shoes and stockings than by young gentlemen riding home on horseback or in coaches to enjoy their Christmas idleness." Nor were the higher mathematics neglected. Spherical trignometry and map projection were a part of the stock-in-trade of schoolmasters in sea-port towns; young men destined for commissions in the army were taught ballistics and surveying; while those entering industry could obtain some knowledge of the natural sciences.

It would be untrue to suggest that the standard in all schools was high. Nevertheless it was high enough in some to produce such famous mathematicians as James Thomson who became professor of mathematics in Glasgow University and who received his early education in Ballynahinch; James McCullagh, son of a small farmer of Glenellie, who became professor of mathematics in Trinity College in 1836 at the early age of twenty-five; Robert Murphy, son of a Mallow shoemaker, who graduated third wrangler in Cambridge in 1829; and John Tyndall, born in Co. Carlow in 1820 and elected Fellow of the Royal Society in 1855.

In later life Tyndall declared that the most important discipline of his days at the school of John Conwill at Ballinabranagh was the study of English grammar. He told the students of University College, London: "The piercing through the involved and inverted sentences of *Paradise Lost,* the linking of the verb to its often distant nominative, of the relative to its transitive verb, of the preposition to the noun or pronoun which it governed, the study of variations in mood or tense, the transpositions often necessary to bring out the true grammatical structure of a sentence, all this was to my young mind a discipline of the highest value and a source of unflagging delight." In the face of this evidence for the intensive study of the text of an English classic it is strange to find that one of the chief grounds of official complaint against the popular schools was that they corrupted the minds of the children by "books calculated to incite to lawless and profligate adventure, to cherish superstition, or to lead to dissention or disloyalty." There were, of course, at this time no school texts for reading. Children brought to school any book they could find at home. It might be the bible, or it might be a tattered copy of *Moll Flanders* or the *History of Freeney the Robber.* It would be easy therefore to collect in the schools a number of books most unsuitable for children. It would be false to represent them as giving the general level of culture.

There were several factors which helped to maintain high standards. Public support naturally went to the able and conscientious master, and parents had more say in deciding the curriculum of a school in that age of private enterprise than they have to-day. There was, too, a fair sprinkling of scholars throughout the country, men who knew something of the cultural standards of Europe; priests who had been trained at Rome, Paris or Louvain; Church of Ireland ministers who were graduates of Trinity; presbyterian clergymen who had attended the ancient universities of Scotland. These helped to kindle the love of learning in many a young breast.

But equally significant and certainly more widespread was the Gaelic tradition of scholarship handed down through the centuries by hereditary scholar families. Though the land confiscations had cut away the economic basis of the system the families still continued to produce scholars and poets who often turned school-master to earn a livelihood. The Kerry poet, Eoghan Ruadh Ó Súilleabháin, the Clare poet, Brian Merriman, the South Armagh poets, Peadar Ó Doirnín and Muiris Ó Gorman, all belonged to this class.

Nowhere had the land confiscations been more thorough than in County Derry. The grocers, drapers, haberdashers and other companies of the City of London had ousted the Ó Cahans, the Mac Gilligans, the Ó Mullans, the Ó Crillys and the rest. Yet the Gaelic tradition was as strong, if not stronger, in County Derry at the beginning of the nineteenth century as in any other county of Ireland. Let us look at the evidence of an unbiassed observer, the Reverend Mr. Ross, rector of Dungiven. He gave a remarkable account of the position in that parish in 1814. He stated that there was then no public or endowed school in the parish but that every townland had at least one school conducted by what he called "the native Irish". The feature which most distinguished the native from the descendant of the Scots settler was, in his opinion, the superior literary taste and lively fancy of the former. "Even in the wildest districts", he wrote, "it is not unusual to meet with young mountaineers whose knowledge and taste in the Latin poets might put to the blush many who have all the advantages of established schools and regular instruction." He gave a sample of the work of one of these young mountaineers—the first ode of Horace done into English verse by a lad of eighteen—Paul McLoskie.

Nor was the native tongue forgotten, Irish, even old Irish, was studied with critical scholarship and the bardic tales were the objects of popular enthusiasm. Mr. Ross continues: "The poems attributed to Ossian, and other bardic remains, are still repeated here by the old seanachies with visible exultation. Eight of them have been written down at my request by a young mountaineer named Bernard MacLoskie, from whose acquaintance with the native traditions, customs and language, the writer derived much assistance in this survey. He is himself a good Latin scholar and possesses, by every account, a critical knowledge of the ancient Irish . . . The manner of preserving the accuracy of tradition is singular and worthy of notice. In the winter evenings a number of Seanachies frequently meet together and recite alternately their traditional stories. If any one repeats a passage which appears to another to be incorrect he is immediately stopped when each gives a reason for his way of reciting the passage; the dispute is then referred to a vote of the meeting and the decision of the majority becomes imperative on the subject for the future."

This was surely something very like a Court of Poetry at work in County Derry in the nineteenth century.

Twenty years later John O'Donovan came to Dungiven but found no trace of it. Sometime in between, "on some wintry night perhaps," to quote Daniel Corkery, "its few remaining old gabblers of verse rose up and bade each other good-night, thinking to meet again, thinking a vain thought." But their spirit lived on. O'Donovan met many inspired by the Gaelic tradition of scholarship, teachers, farm labourers, stone masons. There was, for example, Brian Mann O'Mullan living in a hut on the hillside near Maghera who had a number of Irish MSS.; there was John O'Crilly of Ballynian who was able to tell him the Irish names of all the townlands in Tamlaght O'Crilly; there was Donogh Roe Kenna, Harry McGuigan, Patrick O'Hagan, and last, but by no means least, another McLoskey, John McLoskey, whom he described as "a man of vast erudition." John McLoskey was a schoolmaster, and his reputation continued to be known far beyond County Derry for another generation.

The McLoskeys were hereditary erenaghs, i.e. stewards, of church lands in this county. Right down through the penal days they supplied an unbroken line of parish priests to Dungiven. It was men such as John McLoskey, inheritors of a centuries old tradition, who supplied the teaching power for the popular schools. In this they were sustained and supported by their kinsmen in the church. The organised Catholic Church, just emerging from the penal days, was as yet in no position to challenge directly the Protestant monopoly of official education, though it was pushing forward unobtrusively with its work of establishing schools. The first diocesan seminary was opened at Carlow in 1790 and was quickly followed by others at Kilkenny, Killarney and Belfast. Maynooth College was founded in 1795. In 1814 the Jesuits emerged from the obscurity of the back streets of Dublin, where they had been working for the education of the poor from 1750 onwards, to open Clongowes Wood College. Nanno Nagle had begun her work for the poor children of Cork in 1793; the Christian Brothers' first school was opened at Waterford in 1802; and by 1825 several orders of nuns, the Presentation sisters, the Ursulines, the Poor Clares, the Carmelites, were educating some six thousand girls. All told, however, they did not touch one-fiftieth of the children who needed education nor had the Church the resources to extend their work.

Some form of State aid was necessary before there could be a system of national education. In the circumstances of the time the State did not even contemplate the idea of assisting the Catholic Church to conduct its own schools, nor was it, at the beginning of the nineteenth century, ready itself to accept full responsibility for national education. For a time a compromise solution was found in the Kildare Place Society which resembled those public corporations with which we have since become so familiar. Supported by government grants, directed by the governing class, through it the government could mould public opinion without accepting responsibility for its actions.

The Society, founded in 1811, was the first body in the history of Irish education to introduce the idea of undenominational religious teaching. At first sight this seemed a fair and reasonable approach to a very thorny problem, much superior to that of the avowedly proselytising societies. Parliament voted it £6,980 in 1815, the grant rose year by year until in 1831 it had reached the figure of £30,000. But as its activities extended it came more and more in conflict with Catholic teaching. In 1820, O'Connell and other Catholics left the Society, and in 1825 a Royal Commission reported adversely on its work, stating that is fundamental principles "rested on a compromise, the terms of which they have never been able perfectly to realise, and which, even if realised, not person is of opinion would have been completely satisfactory."

The next approach by the government to the education problem was announced in Ocober, 1831, when the Chief Secretary for Ireland, the Hon. E. G. Stanley, sent his famous letter to the Duke of Leinster. In this he proclaimed the government's intention to establish a National Board of Education, and while the letter explicitly rejected the principle of the Kildare Place Society it declared that the Board would subsidise mixed or united education to the exclusion of schools based on definite religious principles. The mixed school was to be as far as possible under mixed local direction which in turn was to be subject to a mixed Board of Education. There would, however, he separate religious instruction for the children of each denomination at times to be arranged with their pastors.

The Board was immediately attacked by some Church of Ireland bishops on two main grounds: (1) because it deprived that Church of its statutory right to superintend national education (this was a reference to the parish school legislation of Henry VIII); and (2) because it excluded the Bible from the schools. The Presbyterian Church also assailed it, the *Orthodox Presbyterian* writing that it was "the most cunning, the most daring, the most specious attempt that has been made against Protestantism since the day of James II." Many of the Catholic bishops, on the other hand, gave a guarded approval to the scheme. Dr. Doyle of Kildare and Leighlin pointed out that at least it gave priests power to give religious instruction to children of their own flock. Archbishop McHale of Tuam, however, vigorously opposed the Board all his life.

The Board at first consisted of seven members of whom three, the Duke of Leinster, the Archbishop of Dublin, Dr. Whately, and Dr. Franc Sadleir, belonged to the Church of Ireland; two were Catholics, Dr. Murray, Archbishop of Dublin, and Mr. A. R. Blake; and two were Presbyterians, the Rev. Mr. Carlile and Mr. J. Holmes. An annual parliamentary grant was placed at its disposal and it was empowered to assist local committees to build schools, to publish and edit school texts, to pay inspectors, to train teachers and to augment teachers' salaries. Teachers were still allowed to charge fees, but in 1849 an inspector reported that the average income from fees and salary grant of a principal teacher in the comparatively prosperous counties of North-East Ulster was only nine shillings a week.

This estimate of a teacher's worth was perhaps a measure of the value which the Board put on the education to be provided in its schools. If in most places the schools rose to levels of attainment far beyond that planned for them it was because the miserably under-paid teachers took a higher view of their calling than did the Board. But while it is easy to condemn the Board's illiberal attitude it must be remembered that it was contending with difficulties which might have baffled archangels let alone archbishops.

The religious difficulties have already been indicated. On the educational side there was the old Tory attitude, the spirit of the Charter schools, that children of the poor should only be given that education which would fit them for lives of manual labour. This attitude is reflected in the speech of the Rector of Ballymena at a school prize-giving in that town in 1869 when he said: "I greatly feared that the National Schools would prove to be educational hotbeds for stimulating to an undue

QUEEN'S COLLEGE, GALWAY

and morbid extent the intellects of children . . .
Gradually these apprehensions have vanished."

But perhaps at no point was the Board more out of
touch with the aspirations of the mass of the Irish
people than in its attitude to the national question.
Those verses that used to hang in every National School
epitomised the Board's ideals:

> "I thank the goodness and the grace
> That on my birth have smiled,
> And made me in these Christian days
> A happy English child."

It was undoubtedly a debased currency which the
Board offered to the Irish people in its schools, and,
as in economics bad money drives out good, so the
National Schools gradually displaced the small classical
schools of the countryside. In 1867, after thirty-five
years of National education the people of Newtown-
stewart, Co. Tyrone, addressed a memorial to the
Commissioners in which they stated: "We forward a
list of more than 20 teachers who have actually imparted classical instruction since the year 1800 in this
parish . . . At present, with some 25 National Schools
in the parish there is no classical or other superior
education whatever." And the President of All Hallows
College told a Royal Commission in 1855 of the sorrow-
ful fate of the hedgeschool masters. He said: "The
famine nearly eliminated classical education; and the
better class of farmers who used to procure such
education for their children has been broken down or
has emigrated. The smaller classical schools are nearly
all gone; the masters were in many instances obliged
to take refuge in the poor house or on the public
works."

Many tributes have been paid to the popular Irish

schools but there is none more eloquent than that of the Presbyterian divine, Dr. Henry Cooke, who recalled his days at a Co. Derry hedgeschool in these words: "I once had a Roman Catholic companion and I can testify that though loaded with satchel and ornamented with shining morning face we never crept like snail unwillingly to school. He was my senior, nominally my chum but really my teacher. And in Summer we reclined among the purple heather, and the music of the bee was around us while we tended the peaceful flocks with Virgil or fought again the battles of Homer. But when the weather was cold we deserted the open heath, and took refuge under a widespreading hawthorn. It was not a pigmy bush; it was a lovely tree, vast and umbrageous, the growth of centuries. No matter from what point the wind blew it furnished us a welcome and a shelter. Years rolled away but I never forgot our rural study, for it was united with every classical recollection that still adhered to memory."

How admirably that tribute reflects the imponderables of education, those gifts of the spirit which cannot be measured in terms of the statistical subjects so dear to the heart of bureaucracy.

V

THE ARMY

BY R. B. MCDOWELL

THE REVOLUTIONARY AND Napoleonic wars which together lasted with a short break for over twenty years were no exception to the general rule that a great war usually leaves a large literary legacy. As far as the British Isles were concerned most of the literature relating to these wars was the work of professional soldiers writing mainly for professionals, the most outstanding example of course being Wellington's despatches, a wonderful display of techincal competence expressed in clear, crisp, concise prose. And even Napier in his great narrative of the war in the Peninsula rarely relaxed from his severe concentration on technical detail. It was an Irish author, William Hamilton Maxwell, who first realised that the intense enthusiasm of the fiction reading public—a rapidly growing class— for the exploits of the heroes of the Peninsula and Waterloo had created a market which he felt he could satisfy. Maxwell, after probably spending some years on active service himself, had taken orders and had been presented to a living in the west of Ireland where he had few Protestant parishioners and plenty of fishing and shooting. In his first successful book, *The wild sports of the West*, the military motif is discernible, for the narrator is a retired army officer with a stock of military anecdotes. In his later works he found he had struck an inexhaustible vein. Perhaps the best criticism of his approach is contained in a eulogy of his books by Lever, which unconsciously reveals the limitations of Maxwell's approach. In Maxwell's works Lever explains are displayed "the pride, pomp and circumstances of glorious war". There "you feel indeed, the shock of battle, the lowering smoke, the booming gun, the rattling hail of musketry, the tramp, the clash, the crush of charging cavalry, the very din and tumult, the cheer of victory, the yell of triumph are all heard". Maxwell does not indeed ignore the horrors of war, but fundamentally he sees it as a series of glorious exploits performed by high spirited heroes and gentlemen. Lever both admired and imitated him with even greater success. Admittedly Lever had never been in the forces, but the life of a hard riding dispensary doctor in the Irish countryside resembled in some ways active service. And both in Ireland and in his wanderings abroad Lever had had plenty of contact with military and half-pay society. He had a lively imagination and a romantic disposition. Above all he was a happy and vigorous conversationalist, a discerning collector of anecdote, and his early novels are largely conversation poured out on paper. As military life was a fertile source of anecdote both gay and gallant, Lever's material as well as his temperament turned him, for a time into a military novelist. His first two novels dealt largely with garrison life. His third, *Charles O'Malley*, was an expansive study of a soldier's life in the great war. Battle scenes painted with spirit in the grand conventional romantic style, were interspaced with amusing fun behind the lines. And by moving about his hero with some disregard of the probabilities Lever managed to describe Waterloo, the grand climax of his story in the first person from both sides of the field. Lever's novels, put together in a harumscarum fashion, have no doubt their inadequacies. But with their vigorous gusto and candid expression of simple emotions they accurately reflected the spirit of the contemporary soldier. It was not I think altogether accidental that both Maxwell and Lever were Irishmen. Irish social life was still dominated by the landed gentlemen and the Irish gentleman living a less trammelled and settled life than his English equivalent tended to develop in an extreme degree the qualities traditionally associated with his caste. Easy-going and quick-witted, generous and hospitable, he was expected to be skilled in fields sports, jealous of his honour and careless about his debts. A man who knew this soceity and enjoyed its life was easily able to grasp many aspects of military life and would instinctively profoundly respect the soldier.

Leaving this rather speculative ground a cursory glance at the dry evidence of statistics will show the importance of the army in Irish life. There was always a large garrison in the country. At one stage during the French war it was said that there were thirty-two thousand regular troops in Ireland. In addition to the regulars there were the militia and the Yeomanry. The Irish militia which at one time was twenty-one thousand strong, has been recently the subject of a careful study by Sir Henry MacAnally. Each county had to raise a battalion by a sort of modified conscription, recruits being selected by ballot. The militia was not obliged to serve outside the United Kingdom, so except in the year 1798 its record was a placid one of marches and camps. When peace came the militia was disembodied but the permanent staff of each battalion, some officers, N.C.O's and bandsmen were maintained in the county town. The yeomanry were of course volunteers whose duties were limited to attending occasional drills and of acting when called upon. The corps were raised and officered by the local gentry, and about 1830 comprised eleven hundred officers and thirty-five thousand men. As they were bound to be influenced by local prejudices, were scarcely likely to be properly disciplined and were regarded by liberals at any rate as armed conservative bands, they were naturally rather unpopular. So in 1834 Lord Grey's government ordered the disbandment of the Irish yeomanry.

But in spite of the disappearance of the Irish militia and yeomanry there was a large military force in Ireland. After Waterloo the British army was cut down from over two hundred thousand to a little over one hundred thousand men; of this force at least half was abroad, in India and the colonies, of the remainder, nearly half was usually stationed in Ireland. Or to put it another way, there were normally over twenty thousand regulars stationed in Ireland. The size of the Irish garrison of course varied with social and political conditions. In 1847 and 1848 it numbered twenty-seven thousand, and in 1841 at the end of the whig era of conciliation it had dropped to eleven thousand. Since regiments normally served only for a few years at a time in Ireland, and since the military stations were numerous, military movements were very frequent. Thackeray, rather exasperated by overcrowded public coaches and cars, said the Irish were a restless people, always hurrying from place to place. He might have said the same of the soldiery, for regiments and detachments with their baggage trains were frequently moving along the Irish roads (until after the middle of the century of course the railways in Ireland were of little importance). Incidentally, and this may sound rather surprising, when the twentieth foot were marching from Boyle to Dublin during the summer of 1818 they found the Irish summer so sultry that each day they started

70

at two or three in the morning and finished their march before midday.

Moreover, not only was there a comparatively large force in Ireland but many Irishmen joined the army. At one extreme there was the great duke himself and a number of his lieutenants in the Peninsula—Beresford, from County Waterford, who at Albuera had covered himself with glory as a soldier if not as a general and who later by a rare mixture of organizing ability and geniality turned the Portuguese army into a very effective force; Packe who commanded a brigade at Waterloo; Lowry Cole whose monument dominates Enniskillen, Stewart the brother of Lord Castlereagh, a fine cavalry officer who later tried to use cavalry tactics in diplomacy and politics without much success; Sir John Doyle who assisted Beresford in building up the Portuguese army and in later years flung himself into Portuguese politics on the liberal side with more zeal than discretion; Vandeleur who took command of the cavalry at Waterloo when Anglesea was compelled to leave the field; Sir William Ponsonby who led the splendid and decisive charge of the union brigade with such impetuous zeal that he was cut off and killed by the French lancers, his cousin Sir Frederick Ponsonby, colonel of the Light Dragoons who was severely wounded when covering the retreat of the remnants of the Union Brigade, and Gough who after distinguished services in the Peninsula was called out of retirement thirty years later to take command in the Sikh wars. Though his Tipperary tactics, as the newspapers called them, were not very successful, he managed to win a decisive victory just before Sir Charles Napier, who had been sent out to India to supersede him, arrived. Incidentally the Napiers, that brilliant group of brothers, were brought up at Celbridge. At the other extreme were the thousands who enlisted in the ranks. Though it is hard to give a precise figure it is clear that the number of Irishmen serving in Wellington's armies in the Peninsula was high. From the Irish militia alone drafts of several thousands went into the regulars, and we know that the colonel who acted as general recruiting agent in Ireland during the early years of the century handled enormous sums of money for after his death a special inquiry was held into his accounts which he had avoided submitting to the government, and over three hundred thousand pounds was found unaccounted for. Later, from 1830 Ireland was supplying four thousand recruits a year to the army, about one-third of the total intake. This figure does not of course include the Irishmen who enlisted in England. As a result of this large influx of Irishmen, not only the regiments usually associated with Ireland, but many British regiments had a high proportion of Irishmen in their ranks. One of these regiments was the seventy-seventh, and its band-master, O'Connor by name, called a regimental quick march he composed shortly before the Crimean war, "Paddy's Resource".

Before discussing the duties the army performed in Ireland, it is perhaps advisable to consider what sort of an army it was. The British regular army during the first half of the nineteenth century, was an institution which had of course slowly evolved, and it was still the pre-Crimean, the pre-Cardwellian army. If the officer's social status was good and his life often gay, it should not be forgotten that his pay was low and his prospects often bad. Commissions were still sold, and for those who could not afford to purchase, promotion was slow and the great block in promotion which followed the end of the Napoleonic wars meant elderly lieutenants and grey-headed captains. As for the men in the ranks,

Wellington's harsh descriptions are well known. Though it has to be remembered that Wellington who was fortunate enough to combine aristocratic breeding, a strong sense of duty, and the highest ability, was not sympathetic to human frailties. Moreover he was a pessimist with a profound belief in the value of discipline which he believed had turned the British armies he commanded into most effective instruments of war. And in emphasising its importance he was perhaps inclined to deprecate unduly the material he had to work on. Nevertheless about the middle of the century a candid expert on recruiting, giving evidence before a parliamentary commission had to admit that usually only men who could not find other forms of employment went into the army. This is scarcely surprising for the life of a soldier was hard even by working class standards. Pay was low and could be reduced by stoppages, uniforms were often shoddy, for the colonel was still responsible for clothing his regiment, and his pay was fixed on the assumption he could make a profit on it. Discipline was harsh and enforced by frequent floggings. Barrack accommodation on the whole was bad. In Ireland where there were over one hundred barracks. Of these a number dated from the eighteenth century, many of them having been built in its last decade, and this burst of barrack building which was of course caused by the war continued into the early nineteenth century, when money was poured out not only on the construction of barracks, but on coast defence, forts being erected to cover the approaches to Dublin and Cork and the northern bays. On the whole the Irish barracks were often overcrowded, and in the badly ventilated barrack rooms the soldiers' wives and children were accommodated along with the men. Conditions admittedly were slowly improving. In the early twenties, Gough, a first rate regimental officer, when his regiment, the twenty-second, was stationed at Cork, began to award good-conduct badges. Ten years later the practice was sanctioned by the War Office and good-conduct gratuities added. Savings-banks, games and libraries were being introduced from the thirties, and humanitarian sentiment managed to secure the substitution in most instances of imprisonment for flogging.

If the soldier was miserably housed and paid he was at least sumptuously dressed. During the Napoleonic wars if uniforms were bright they were in cut at least fairly practical. And often under exigencies of campaigning many of the niceties of dress were lost. For instance when in 1798 the bulk of the Royal Lancashire Militia volunteered to cross to Ireland, those who refused to budge were there and then stripped of their kit for the benefit of their inadequately equipped fellow soldiers. And a drawing of an Irish corporal of the eighty-eighth in the Peninsula shows him with a shapeless shako and a ragged uniform comfortably adapted to his build. But with the war over the fantasies of the regency could have full play. The British army was to be dressed as befitted a victorious force which was expected to provide the pageantry requisite to the dignity of the state. Uniforms became more brilliant than ever, the basic colours being set off by bright facings and overlaid with gold lace. The military coat became tight, elongated, narrow waisted and top-heavy. In the case of the infantry, the short shako of the Peninsula was replaced by the heavy bell-shaped one heavily ornamented with metal. As for the cavalry their head-dresses, bearskins or helmets were fantastically elaborate and dangerously liable to fall off. Admittedly an era of pruning came in at the end of

George IV's reign, perhaps the most noticeable change being the introduction of the simpler Prince Albert shako in the forties. But even after the Crimean war the army remained brightly coloured in an age when men's clothing was steadily sobering down.

We must now turn to the work of the army in Ireland. Most of the soldier's time was of course spent in the daily round of peace time routine, drills, parades, fatigues and marches. But as Peel, when Chief Secretary, explained the troops stationed in Ireland were expected to fulfil three functions, their ordinary military duties, assisting the civil power in preserving the public peace, and thirdly to suppress illicit distillation, a grievous bane to Ireland. Until Drummond's reorganization reforms were effected in the late thirties, the Irish Police forces (of which there were several) were weak and ineffective. Moreover throughout the early nineteenth century the heavy burdens which oppressed a distressed peasantry produced frequent agrarian disturbances. Severity on the part of the landlord or the tithe owner was answered by agrarian conspiracy and popular coercion often directed against innocent and lowly victims. During the twenties these disturbances became exceedingly serious in Munster and in the early thirties a general strike against tithe spread across the south and west. Aiding the civil power imposed on the army a constant series of unpleasant duties. It involved supplying detachments to escort prisoners, to protect sub-sheriffs executing judgments against defaulting tenants and tithe payers, to guard wrecks, to keep the peace at fairs and race meetings, to stop Orange processions and take down Orange arches, and to search the country for arms. As a result regiments were frequently split up in numerous small detachments, scattered at different posts, there being at one time no fewer than four hundred military stations in Ireland. And it says a great deal for discipline and for the men themselves that very few complaints were made against their behaviour. On the whole the appearance of the military with their precision of movement and their glittering accoutrements had a salutary effect. In one sense at any rate. It often prevented that spasmodic and unco-ordinated violence which could only have caused arbitrary suffering. Sometimes the use of force was merely absurd as when large detachments were sent out to assist in the collection of tithe. They would lumber along the country lanes, sometimes threatened by angry crowds, always impeded by legal complications, and often baffled by the countryman's cleverness. A few times during the half century the threat of insurrection was in the air. An hussar officer has left us some irritated reminiscences of the rebellion in Munster in 1848 from the soldier's point of view. He tells how for three weeks his regiment had to retire to bed in their overalls booted and spurred, how every night their sleep was broken and they sat for hours freezing on their horses waiting further orders, and how all the time they were told they must on no account give any provocation or fire first. The troubles besetting military men in a time of stress is illustrated in another way by the well publicized episode of Mr. Maher's lawn. In August 1848 Maher, the well-known liberal M.P. for Tipperary wrote a most indignant letter to the Secretary of War complaining that according to his agent the 85th had pitched their camp on the lawn in front of his house. He admitted that the state of excitement in Ireland might palliate taking possession for military purposes of a remote part of his demesne, but he declared with that magnificent respect for the rights of the respectable characteristic of the day, that to enter on a man's best land and surround his pleasure garden with a thousand soldiers was an outrage which could not be tolerated even if martial law was proclaimed. In a second letter, written a few days later he added that his agent had informed him that the military were billeting horses in his stables, and that General McDonald's savage temper made it useless to speak to him about it. The army officers concerned were quick to make a counter-case. The troops referred to (five hundred and seventy-one, not a thousand strong) had been moved into a badly cut field some distance from the house. As for the stables Mr. Maher's servants had been quite willing to allow them to be used, and the only disputes, which had been financial, had been satisfactorily settled. Unfortunately, as so often happens in history the truth will never be known.

Another form of police work the army had to perform was trying to keep order at elections. For instance in 1835 no fewer than one hundred and fifty detachments were moved to points where it was feared political exuberance might develop into violence. And in the general election of 1841 which was not an outstandingly stormy one, in Belfast both infantry and hussars were out patrolling the streets, in Cork dragoons and infantry had to be rushed up to prevent a house being demolished and in Carlow lancers were used to escort conservative electors to the polls. At the beginning of the century troops stationed in Ireland were kept busy still hunting as it was termed. Their duty was to protect the revenue officers when making seizures and it could be exciting, one party for instance in wild country having to fire two hundred rounds, relinquish their seizures, take refuge in a house and wait to be relieved by a detachment which was two hundred strong. Troops engaged in this work were paid at the rate of half a guinea an officer, half a crown a sergeant, and one and eight pence a private. And an experienced N.C.O. was careful to point out that the full amount had to be paid if the party spent an hour away at least a mile from barracks. The military authorities thought the use of troops for this purpose bad for discipline and from 1817 discouraged it, with the result that enterprising revenue officers built up irregular bands for their own protection. In 1835 these bands were fused into the revenue police and placed under the command of Colonel Brereton, a strict disciplinarian, who discovered that light infantry drill could be easily adapted to still hunting.

As this point I want to say a word on an aspect of military life which is not revealed in the high-spirited novels of Lever, the contribution the army made to the administrative system. At the beginning of the nineteenth century the civil service was badly planned and badly manned. One of the most interesting features of the period is the emergence of the modern civil service with strict selection of personnel, definition of functions, regularity and uniformity. Now the army officer was accustomed to managing men, knew the meaning of discipline and was aware of the perplexities involved in running a large-scale organization. When in 1835 Gosset, who had been a colonel in the engineers was transferred to England, he was succeeded as Under-Secretary for Ireland by that remarkable man, Thomas Drummond, who combined great administrative drive with strong liberal opinions. Drummond, an officer in the engineers had learned about Irish conditions when engaged in the Ordnance survey. His aim as Under-Secretary, was to uphold a policy of firmness and fair play. One of his instruments in this was the reformed police force which was disciplined and organized by

two Peninsular veterans, General Shaw Kennedy and
and Colonel McGregor. Another instrument was the
resident magistrates, several of whom were army
officers. Some years before Drummond took office
General Burgoyne, a future field marshal, was appointed
chairman of the Irish board of works. The author of
an anonymous pamphlet advocating a reduction of
rents, he tried to use public works as an instrument of
social policy. Still another officer interested in Irish
conditions was Pitt Kennedy, secretary of the Devon
commission which carried out a great survey of Irish
agrarian life. Lastly I might mention commissary general
Routh who organized relief during the famine, and
Renny, an army surgeon who was a pioneer in social
medicine. But perhaps I may conclude on a less serious
note. The army was also a social force in the less
austere sense of the term. Parades and military bands,
the private swaggering off duty or the mounted orderly
enlivened urban life, and on the sovereign's birthday
the Dublin garrison would carry out in the Park
elaborate military manoeuvres—a march past of horse,
foot and artillery, followed by a sham fight. And even
a small garrison could stage something. For instance
the fifty-seventh being stationed at Galway on George
IV's coronation day paraded, fired a *feu de joie* and
gave three cheers for the king. Then the men and women
of the regiment sat down to a dinner provided by the
officers. As for the life of an officer stationed in Ireland,
Lever declares it was spent in dining, drinking, dancing,
riding, steeple-chasing, pigeon shooting, tandem driving,
garrison balls and garrison plays. And Ross-Lewin who
was a subaltern in the thirty-second early in the century
says that when his regiment was stationed in Galway
there was such a continuous round of conversaziones,
tea and card parties that the ladies wore their silk
stockings the whole time.

BY K. H. CONNELL

IN THE EARLY 1840s more than eight million people lived in Ireland. So large a population, twice that of the present day, had been achieved after a period of rapid growth. But we have no trustworthy figures to tell us how rapid the growth had been, or how prolonged: the first census was not taken until 1821 and the estimates of earlier years may lead us far astray. That for 1785 puts the population at under three million; there is little doubt that it must be raised by a full million, and probably by more. But we must not forget that the four million, or more, of 1785 were the progenitors not only of the eight million of 1845, but also of the two million who had moved to Britain or America in the intervening years.

We can thus do little more than guess at the dimensions of our problem. But we can be certain that at some time in the decades before the Famine the divergence between the birth and the death rates widened and that continuously there was an unusually large excess of births over deaths. But, unfortunately, we shall never be able to assess the relative contributions of rising fertility and falling mortality. We shall never know by how much the birth rate rose or the death rate fell since it was not for twenty years after the Famine that the state required the registration of births and deaths. Lacking vital statistics, we can only grope

FOURTH or ROYAL IRISH DRAGOON GUARDS

FICER, FOURTH OR ROYAL IRISH DRAGOON GUARDS, 1838

for what seems to be the most likely explanation of the vigour of population growth: we can never be certain that the explanation for which we opt is, in fact, the correct one.

Our most promising procedure, I think, is by trial and error. There is only a limited number of ways in which it is at all probable that fertility rose or mortality fell. If we appraise each in the light of what we know of social and economic conditions we may hope that some will seem so incongruous that we may disregard them, while the aptness of others will persuade us that they hold our secret.

Turning first to the possible causes of higher fertility, the logician or the biologist could point to a number which are Aunt Sallies to the historian of early nineteenth century Ireland. There is, I think, only one that can survive his sticks: this is the possibility that the birth rate rose because the proportion of women who were married, and therefore likely to have children, encroached upon the population who were unmarried, and almost certainly childless.

Now, if this happened, it is probably the result of one or both of two processes. It might have followed a change in women's conduct—more of them wanted, or were able, to marry. Or, on the other hand, it might have been a mechanical consequence of an increase in proportion of women of marriageable age—there were more marriageable women, therefore there were more married women.

Let us look first at this second point. We shall argue presently that population began to grow rapidly around 1780 largely because of an increase in the number of children. If we are correct, then some fifteen or twenty years after this initial impetus, as the children who caused it grew up and married, they inflated the proportion of married women. More married women, in turn meant more children: thus there was a new factor reinforcing or replacing the original cause of the growth of population. And for all we know the process continued cumulatively until the Famine.

It appears, then, that in the very process of population growth there is a significant cause of the vigour of that growth. But we cannot demonstrate—and it certainly is not probable—that this internal source of energy was ever the sole source; and, logically, it could not have been the initial source. We must, then, revert to the other possible explanation of an increase in the proportion of married women: was it that women became more willing to marry, or had greater opportunity to do so?

There seem to have been too few life-long spinsters for any reduction in their number to have been of much consequence; we must concern ourselves, therefore, with the possibility of a lowering of the age of marriage. We can say, I think, that by the end of the eighteenth century the Irish had long lived in an environment which made them ready to marry young and which left them unaware of the prudential restraints which elsewhere led to the voluntary postponement of marriage. An evil land system ensured that the material condition of the Irish was commonly wretched and hopeless, so hopeless as to make nonsense of the suggestion that marriage be deferred until it improved; so wretched that no one supposed an improvident marriage could depress it, while all saw in the society of a wife the promise of consolation, if not mitigation. But the upward trend in the population curve does not appear to have coincided with any deterioration in social conditions, nor with any greater impatience to marry: it did coincide, I suggest, with new opportunities to gratify an impatience long-felt. Marriage, in a peasant community, presupposed the finding of a "settlement", the land, or the job on the land, which could give some pretence of providing for a new family. Settlements had been scarce; but now changes in the rural economy made them available to all; now men could marry when they wished, not after a long wait for dead men's shoes.

We can see, I think, the sort of thing that happened by analogy with modern Ireland. Farms, to-day are usually passed on intact from father to son. When the father dies, or feels his active days have passed, the "boy" takes over the farm. The transfer is made when the father is perhaps sixty-five or seventy; the son, therefore, is likely to be thirty or thirty-five. But the son waits until his thirties, not only to acquire a farm, but to acquire also a wife. He is, of course, formally free to marry before, but he is dissuaded from doing so because the tradition lingers on that when a father chooses to endow his son with the family land, he chooses also his bride; a son who denied the patriarch the crowning display of his authority might find that he had denied himself the land; he *could* find himself homeless, and it would be a foolhardy bride whom he could tempt to come to his home and dispute his mother's authority. Now, men who marry when they are approaching thirty-five are apt to marry women already in their thirties. And a woman who marries when she is over thirty is likely to have fewer children that a woman who marries at, say twenty.

It is this postponement of marriage, dictated by the system of family farming, that seems to be the chief cause of the relatively small families to be found to-day in the Irish countryside. And I suggest (though I should be hard put to find an approach to proof for every step in the argument)—I suggest that for the greater part of the eighteenth century the rural economy raised some similar obstacle to marriage; that changes in this economy, dating from about the 1780s made settlements available for all; that men and women who could now marry when they pleased, were pleased to marry younger than their parents, and found themselves, in consequence, with larger families than they.

In the eighteenth century the landlords' obsessive pre-occupation with the size of their rents at once hindered and impelled agricultural change. It hindered the intro-duction of more productive methods by smothering principles of estate-management that might have made farming more prosperous and rents more secure; it robbed the tenants of the incentive and the capital that make progressive farmers. But at the same time, by making rent the one restless element in an otherwise sluggish economy it stirred it to some movement. Because of the pressure of rent the peasant found that the land producing his rent tended continuously to encroach on the land producing his food. This fact, to my mind, must dominate any analysis of the economy of Ireland in the eighteenth century; it lay behind the wretched, hopeless lives which have already found a place in our argument; it is a partial, if not essential, explanation of the Irishman's dependence on the potato, the crop which would feed him with the greatest economy of land. With more immediate relevance to our argument, I suggest that it also created a scarcity of settlements which, before the period of rapid population growth, necessitated the postponement of marriage. Given its commitments to the landlord, each peasant family had no more land than would see it fed and clothed. There was none to spare to endow to a second family. However anxious a son might be to marry he could find the settlement which enabled him to do so only when he succeeded to his father's tenancy. But by that time he and his bride were no longer young; and the size of their family, accordingly, was likely to be reduced.

It is curious that the same quest for greater rent which had made settlements scarce in the earlier eighteenth century helped afterwards to make them abundant. Traditionally, the peasant had found his rent by the sale of livestock and their products: little grain had been grown. But by the last third of the eigtheenth century several developments were increasing the profit-ability of corn-growing. England no longer had grain to spare for the Irish towns, and now became willing to tolerate legislation which effectively encouraged corn-growing in Ireland; the outbreak of war with France in 1793 sent grain prices soaring for twenty years. And all the time, of course, population was rising: labour was becoming more abundant and land more scarce; it was attractive, therefore, to substitute arable for pasture so as to use more cheap labour and less dear land.

Now, because of the sharp rise in grain prices which had set in in the closing decades of the eighteenth century, tilling tenants found themselves possessed of an unwonted surplus when they had paid their rents and fed their families. It was, therefore, tilling tenants for whom the landlords yearned—so that they might annex this surplus to their rent. That they did not vainly yearn is shown by the very substantial extension of arable farming in the decades after 1780. But (and this is a critical step in our argument) by encouraging arable farming the landlords necessarily encouraged smaller scale farming.

Family-farming was the Irish tradition, and no de-velopment associated with the extension of arable weakened its hold: landlords remained as reluctant as ever to invest in the land; there was no new body of tenants with both the means to embark upon farming on a larger scale and the foolhardiness to risk these resources when tenure was so precarious. Family farming, then, survived the swing towards arable. But the old family farms were by no means preserved intact; when a family grows grain the area with which it can economically cope is smaller than when it keeps stock. And because of this the swing towards arable farming impelled a movement towards smaller scale farming. Moreover (though it might be far-fetched to regard this as a direct influence on the conduct of either landlord or tenant) arable farming needed more labour: it needed, that is, the stimulus to the growth of population given, as we shall presently see, by the reduction in the size of holdings. Nor did the pressure towards smaller farms spring entirely from the exigencies of corn-growing. Sub-division of holdings quickened the rate of population growth, but the faster population grew, the more imperative it became for each family to make do with the least area of land. Cause and effect, here, as elsewhere in our argument, are closely mingled.

Fertility, to summarise this stage of the argument, seems to have been conditioned by the structure of the rural economy. For the greater part of the eighteenth century settlements had been scarce because an ever-advancing rent obliged the peasant family to get its living from a minimal area; an area that would sustain one family but seldom two. As a result the son's marriage had to be delayed until the father was advancing in years; family size, accordingly, was reduced and the growth of population restrained. But by the 1780s the pattern was changing. Rent was as expensive as ever, but new marketing conditions were linking its expansion with the extension of arable farming. Corn-growers could now offer more tempting rents; therefore landlords wanted more of them. But in the circumstances of the time the corn-farm tended to be smaller than the stock-farm it supplanted. The peasant, therefore, found he needed less land; he had, in fact, some to spare to create, or contribute towards, a new holding. Nor was this the only way in which settlements became more abundant: as arable farming required more labour there were more jobs to give what assurance was conventional for the future of a family: there was, too, a vigorous, though piecemeal, attack on the bog and mountainy land. As settlements, for all these reasons, were more easily found, marriage had no longer to be delayed until one's father was senile. The youthfulness of marriage struck every commentator on the social condition of Ireland in the early nineteenth century; and the earlier the marriage the larger the family.

So much for fertility. Now we must try to find if a rising birth rate seems to be the entire explanation of the growth of population, or if its effect was enhanced by that of a falling death rate. Discussion of population growth elsewhere suggests three ways in which mortality in Ireland may have fallen, three fields, therefore, in which we must assess possibilities. First, were the Irish living in a healthier environment, with better houses, purer water and safer drains? The answer, obviously, is no. Second, did the skill of their doctors increase; were there more of them, practising, perhaps, in better hospitals and dispensaries? Hospitals certainly were built; but beyond Dublin they were few and small until after the Famine. The peasant's remedies came to him before the days of scientific medicine: innovations were suspect, and vaccination is probably the only one at all likely to have made an impression on the national death rate.

Our third enquiry centres on nutrition. Were the Irish at the end of the eighteenth century better fed than formerly? Did their number grow so fast because so few of them succumbed to deficiency diseases? I think we can be quite certain that, except in a bad year, the Irish were extraordinarily well fed; and bad years were few until, in the twenties and thirties, foretastes of the disasters of the forties became frequent and widespread. It is, of course, the most striking paradox of the social history of Ireland in the decades around 1800 that a people whose wretchedness was proverbial were remarkably well nourished. The pivot of the paradox is the potato. It yielded food more bountifully than any alternative crop: this (in part) is why the Irish were forced to make it their staple; this also, is why they could consume it with such extravagance. We may believe, on quite indisputable authority, that in years of normal harvests an adult Irishman consumed ten or twelve pounds of potatoes a day. Nor, in a country where butter was still widely made were men wholly without milk—or skim-milk, or butter-milk—to soften their potatoes or wash them down. Assuming that with his ten pounds of potatoes the Irishman had a daily pint of whole milk, then, whatever the scorn of the gourmet, to the biochemist he was almost perfectly nourished. And of what other country, in whatever half-century, could this be said?

Must we, then, regard the nutritional excellence of the Irishman's diet as a stimulus to population growth perhaps no less potent than rising fertility? We could so, I think, only if the critical decade in the history of population was also (or quickly followed) a critical decade in the history of dietaries. But the history of dietaries is not given to crises, save when they are provoked by war or crop-failure; and in the eighteenth century there seems to have been no such catastrophe driving masses of the Irish to make a sudden and lasting substitution of potatoes for gruel. The potato's conquest of the Irishman's board was a piecemeal process spread over a century and a half: a few districts, doubtless, quickly foresook the traditional foods, but elsewhere their retreat was more stubborn and in parts of the north-west the potato supplemented cereals but never supplanted them. No only was the advance of the potato, by and large, a slow process; it was also by 1750 virtually an accomplished process: few of the areas that only dallied with it then ever succumbed to the full. It follows that any tendency of the potato to lower national mortality would have been felt over a long period, and to the full by the middle of the century. It is hard to see how so gradual a development, completed a generation earlier directly contributed to what we picture as a sudden upswing in the population curve.

The potato, I think, must be fitted into our explanation less for what it did than for what it prevented; not because it reduced mortality but because it prevented a rise. We are, after all, discussing an age in which enlightened men accepted Malthus's theory of population and believed with him that the number of people tended to grow more rapidly than the supply of food; they believed that if men and women were misguided enough to use to the full the powers of reproduction with which they were endowed they would soon learn from higher mortality that nature did not provide for their sustenance as liberally as she provided for their reproduction. That these fears had an urgent relevance to Ireland is suggested by the catastrophe of the Famine: then, within a decade, the failure of food supplies reduced by a quarter a population unfortunate enough to have doubled in sixty years. To the Malthusian the problem of the Famine is not why it came, but why it was pent up for the forties. According to Malthus a people multiplying with the abandon of the Irish should have been scourged with early death; scorning his prudential check it should have felt the sting of the positive check. I suggest that the immense contribution of the potato is that for sixty years it delayed the association of high mortality with high fertility.

This, then, as I see it, is the play of population in Ireland before the Famine. Changes in the rural economy in the closing decades of the eighteenth century allowed women to marry younger; they became mothers earlier, and, in consequence, more frequently. Until the 1820s the survival of their children had been ensured by the abundance of the potato, but by then the potato was becoming a precarious support. In the twenty years before 1845 its repeated failure probably cost more lives than were saved by vaccination. But in spite of mounting mortality there remained an impressive excess of births over deaths. That fertility stayed so high must be attributed in part, I think, to its rise a generation earlier: as a result there was now an unusually large number of young people expecting to marry. Some of them, without doubt, found that their father's potato land could be pared no more if he and they were to live. But settlements were to be found elsewhere than on the family's potato land: increasingly mountain and bog were farmed; and increasingly, I suggest, the tenants were appropriating for their own use land which had traditionally earned the rent. Reclamation, of course, was no novelty; but the reversal of the chronic expansiveness of rent land, whenever it took place, is a decisive point in the history of Irish economic life: that it took place, or at least was anticipated, before the Famine is implied by the landlord's laments for rents unpaid, as well as by the history of agrarian outrage.

I said that I was unable to prove every step in my argument. The one that is most rickety—and it is critical to the whole structure—is that women did, in fact, marry earlier towards the end of the eighteenth century. Of this I can offer no proof. The age of the bride is not to be found in the parochial registers and without such information my contention can be supported only by presumption. And that presumption, in this case, may be presumptuous is suggested by Petty's comment a century earlier: Irish women, he said, "marry upon the first capacity". It is true that there is far more comment on the precocity of marriage around 1800 than ever before, but this is no guarantee that it had become more familiar: travellers and journalists, seeking the bizarre, were getting to know that Ireland would not disappoint them; Malthus was making it fashionable to attribute poverty to improvident marriage, and many found it more palatable to seek the salvation of Ireland in the prudence of her people than in the penance of her landlords.

The plausibility of the theory I have outlined is to be found, if anywhere, in the extent to which it explains a novel trend in population in terms of novel developments in the economy. Smaller farms, many of them growing corn, many of them taking in land recently waste: these are the elements that distinguish the economy of Ireland in the decades after 1780; these also, in my argument, are the elements of the peculiar pattern which population assumed in that economy. But we can never be certain that the coincidence is significant: we can never dismiss out of hand alternative explanations of the growth of population. The most attractive, I think, centres on another coincidence: that a people growing remarkably fast was a people fed remarkably well. But the more we emphasise the potato's tendency to lengthen life, the more critical must we be of the idea that the 1780s were decisive years in the history of population. Instead we should believe that the steepening of the population curve was gentler and earlier—early enough to have followed hard on the dissemination of the potato: we should believe, that is, that the eighteenth-century estimates are even more misleading than we have supposed.

VII

THE PRESS

BY BRIAN INGLIS

PERHAPS THE MOST striking thing about the Irish newspapers of the early part of the last century compared with the newspapers of the present day is their dullness. They contain no illustrations, no headlines, few variations of type; just column after column of reports, despatches and articles thrown into the paper with hardly any attempt to "sub-edit" them. The bulk of the material used is foreign; not because editors then were any less parochial in their outlook than they are now, but because the foreign news could be extracted free from the English newspapers when they arrived in Dublin by the post. To obtain Irish news an editor would have to pay somebody; the proportion of Irish news therefore remained very small. Half-a-column of home news out of the standard sixteen-column, four-page paper was a not unusual proportion. The rest of the paper, apart from advertisements, would consist of despatches from the Continent and English news. This was the same whatever might be the paper's politics: but in any case at the time of the Union all the Dublin newspapers were conservative. There were six of them: three owned (in effect) by the Government; one non-political, concentrating almost exclusively on advertisements; and two that had formerly been liberal, with United Ireland sympathies, but had been cowed into respectful submission in 1798. Their combined circulation (though exact figures are not available) cannot have reached five figures; and the only discernible difference between them was that the more liberal papers were a little less turgid, had more advertisements, and printed more home news. Most of it consisted of reports of robberies, arson, murder, executions, and sudden death in all its forms. An exception had been the reports of the Irish Parliament: but after the Union, reports from Westminster, taken from English papers, took their place. And although articles on Irish subjects—politics, or religion—were not uncommon, they usually took the form of a letter to the editor over a pen name, and one cannot help suspecting that the editor wrote many of them to himself. There were editorials, of course, but often they were abominably written. To give an example: "the emolliency of our abominable antipathies, nor even their positive cessation, could not at once work a miracle, and brush away the inveteracies which the habits of long ages had been producing."

The impression given, in fact, by the newspapers of the first quarter of the nineteenth century is often that they were run by a not-very-bright man and a boy. They sometimes were. One man was often owner, editor, manager, leader-writer, accountant, theatre critic, and reporter. Staffs of reporters, sub-editors and so on were unknown.

The predominant impression of dullness, then, is only a reflection of poverty. Poverty of invention, to some extent—because it has to be said that newspapers had been much more interesting before: the *Freeman's Journal* under Lucas and Grattan: the Belfast *Northern Star* under Neilson: and the *Press*, run by the Dublin United Irishmen. But the real poverty was simply lack of funds. And the chief reason for it can be found in the top corner of any copy of a newspaper of those times; a Government stamp, worth twopence. Every copy published had to bear this stamp; and for every copy published, the Irish Treasury was twopence the richer. That was not all. A tax had to be paid on each advertisement printed; a duty had to be paid on the newsprint used; and there were sundry other taxes payable to the State for the privilege of publishing a newspaper. By the time that they had all been paid, it meant that a newspaper could not be sold at much less than fivepence a copy. Fivepence in those days was worth very much more than it is now; it is difficult to compute accurately, but these small, dull newspapers cost the equivalent of about four shillings to-day.

This meant, in the first place, that only a small minority of people bought newspapers. An editor thought himself doing well if he achieved a circulation of over a thousand. But if a newspaper only reaches a small audience, it does not attract advertisers. Advertisers were in any case few, in those days, and they were further discouraged by the advertisement tax—which, of course, the newspapers tried to pass on to them. Without a good revenue from advertisers, it was impossible for the press to expand—to employ more and better writers. And because the newspapers remained badly written and dull, they did not attract more readers. Responsibility for the press's weakness lay, in fact, with the Government—'the Castle,' as it had long been called colloquially, though, after 1800, the decisions were usually taken not in Dublin, but in Whitehall.

To understand the press in this period then, it is necessary first to understand its relation to the government. The press was not thought of at that time—as it was later—as the "Fourth Estate". Governments did not recognise the press as an independent and free entity, existing as a day-to-day mouthpiece of the people.

Admittedly the phrase "the freedom of the press" was bandied about by politicians—just as it often is to-day. But they liked the idea even less, then. Governments looked upon newspapers then rather as they now look upon public relations departments; that is to say, editors were expected to support the Government, and to provide reasons for its decisions. If the Government decreed that black was in future to be white, an editor was expected to announce that this reform was long overdue, and would be welcomed by all thinking people. Editors who performed this service were rewarded. They were given government advertising—very extensive in those days, as the Government took it upon itself to keep people informed of such things as outbreaks of plague in places as far away as Gibraltar, much as they now might announce outbreaks of foot and mouth disease nearer home. Editors (I am using the word "editor", incidentally, to include owners, as they were so often one and the same) would also receive secret-service subsidies for their papers, and pensions for themselves. They might even get "jobs" in the government service for themselves or their relatives as well. Journalists were thought of in much the same terms as barristers are to-day. Just as a barrister who backs the right political party now may get himself a judgeship, so a journalist who backed the right party then might obtain preferment in a variety of ways.

But the trouble with these Government newspapers, as the Castle always found to its annoyance, was that nobody wanted to read them. The reason is obvious: the Castle was not popular. The Union had only been won by the lavish distribution of money and titles; it was no more popular with the Ascendancy as a whole than with the people. Therefore, the editor of a newspaper found himself in a difficult situation. He could, if he wished, come to terms with the Castle. That meant financial security for himself and his family. But it also meant that his readers left his paper and went elsewhere, so that the ridiculous situation arose where there were three or four newspapers praising the Government to a handful of readers. Alternatively, the editor could take his newspaper along an independent line. But if he wanted to attract readers enough to survive, it had to be a strong line, denouncing the Castle for its incompetence or wrong-headedness. This brought in the readers; but it also brought in writs for seditious libel, and before very long the venturesome editor would be behind bars for a spell, there to meditate on how to raise the money to pay a heavy fine.

A typical example came in 1813. John Magee, a young Protestant who was fighting for Catholic Emancipation, had built up the prosperity and reputation of his *Dublin Evening Post* so that it had probably a bigger circulation than all the Castle papers put together. Robert Peel, who had just come over as Chief Secretary, decided that the *Post* must be taught a lesson. With the help of packed juries it was not difficult to get Magee sentenced to two years imprisonment and a fine of £500; and, as that did not silence the *Post,* to add a further six months and £1,000 to his sentence on another charge. The libels in question undoubtedly *were* seditious, from the Castle's point of view; that is to say, they were calculated to arouse violent feelings against the Government. And Daniel O'Connell's speech in Magee's defence, though it is generally conceded to be his finest forensic effort, was not so much a defence of Magee as a defence of the libels—which didn't help Magee. The Government could, and often did, proceed against an independent newspaper in the courts, even if it did not have so good a case. Juries could be packed, and the judges, such as Lord Norbury, were solidly behind the Castle.

Still, these prosecutions, although they attracted a lot of publicity, were not the Government's chief weapon to control the press. In fact when they took place it was really a sign that the Government's control had broken down somewhere. As Richard Brinsley Sheridan told the house of commons in 1811: "there are three ways of destroying the liberty of the press: one is by oppressive acts of parliament; another is by the banishment of printers to distant gaols; and the third is by raising the price of cheap publications. This—and it is the way resorted to in Ireland—is mean and cowardly."

The story of the press in this period is mainly the story of the newspapers' efforts to achieve independence. They had none at the beginning of the period: Castlereagh had seen to that. And Robert Peel, with his belief in what he termed "honest despotism", clamped down upon them again in 1813. But a decisive change came in the early 'twenties, with the arrival of a conciliatory viceroy, Wellesley. The Castle newspapers found their subsidies being withdrawn, and one by one they collapsed. The independent newspaper editors, on the other hand, found that they could express themselves freely on what became the chief issue of the day —Catholic Emancipation. And one of them, forgotten to-day, deserves a nod of friendly recognition. Like Magee, Michael Staunton was a Protestant who had thrown himself into the struggle for Emancipation. He realised that for O'Connell's cause to be spread it must be properly publicised, and he introduced to Ireland the reporter system—at considerable cost to himself. The other newspapers were compelled to follow suit. For the first time, Irish news came to be reported extensively. Staunton was known in his time as the father of the Irish press. He greatly improved the printing of newspapers by setting a high standard in his *Weekly Register* and *Morning Register*, and he did his best to make his staff conscious of their dignity as professional men—not hacks. For example, on the Royal visit to Dublin in 1821, the press were only allotted standing room, outside the premises of the Dublin Society, for a function there. Staunton protested against this "inconvenience and, indeed indignity" and although the omission was hastily rectified, he refused to allow the event to be reported. How valuable his help was to O'Connell is not easy to judge; O'Connell, who resented Staunton's sturdy independence of mind, was often ungrateful. But the *Register* remained the most influential Catholic newspaper until the early forties. Incidentally, it was to give Dillon and Thomas Davis their first schooling in journalism.

Although as influential, in a very different way, was a comic character called Joseph Timothy Haydn, later to be celebrated as the compiler of the *Dictionary of Dates*. He was a Castle hack under Peel, but when Wellesley arrived, Haydn got the idea that an outright Protestant paper, anti-Catholic *and* anti-Emancipation, would sell. With this in mind he founded the *Evening Mail* in Dublin, which suspended publication only in 1961. In its origins it was unblushingly a gutter paper, trading on religious bigotry and accusing the Viceroy of moral turpitude and O'Connell of murder. This line was popular with the Ascendancy, who were beginning to get annoyed with both the Viceroy and O'Connell at the prospect of Emancipation. As juries were drawn exclusively from the Ascendancy, it was useless for the Government to try to prosecute Haydn. But it was not very long before his scurrilities had run him into a series of libel actions taken by individuals.

In such cases the courts were not necessarily on the newspaper's side, and Haydn was soon sacked by the newspaper's owners. But he had started something. Vicious though the *Mail* was in those days, it certainly woke the other newspapers up. Haydn could say about the Editor of the *Morning Post*: "We have shown this imbecile, yet noxious reptile", Haydn wrote, "to be a calumniator and a coward: we must now prove him to be a liar"; to which the *Post* replied calling Haydn a "desperate madman" and a "hangman-headed dog". The controversy might be disreputable but it certainly was not dull.

The *Evening Mail* was not in fact the oldest Irish newspaper: that distinction is held by the *Belfast Newsletter*, which is now well into its third century. Another Belfast paper, the *Northern Whig*, dates from the 1820's, but apart from the *Mail*, the only Dublin paper running in the early nineteenth century which some of you will remember was the *Freeman's Journal*. At the time of the Union it was owned by Francis Higgins, "the Sham Squire", and run as a Castle paper, with a circulation probably, of less than a hundred. But after his death it picked up, becoming a solid and respectable daily concentrating on advertisements. At no time during this period was it influential. Another newspaper which was not as influential as might be expected was O'Connell's mouthpiece, the *Pilot*. It ran from Emancipation time for twenty years, but in spite of the fact that O'Connell lavished attention on it, giving it priority of news, sending it letters, and so on, it never prospered. Its editor was a curious character, Richard Barrett. Like Haydn, he had first tried to ingratiate himself with the Castle—by writing pamphlets against the Catholic cause. In one of them he had this description of O'Connell: "his accent is broad, his language coarse and sterile . . .

there is even a flat vulgarity in his countenance, where one can discern no trait of mental intelligence". When the writer was converted to the Emancipation cause a few years later, O'Connell bore him no grudge, but worked him hard—on more than one occasion, Barrett went to jail for his leader. He was not the only journalist to refuse to give the source of his information and go to jail so that O'Connell might be left free. But the *Pilot* was never a commercial success. It collected only about half the number of readers who bought the rival *Dublin Evening Post*, which by this time had settled down to pursue what would later have been called a "Castle Catholic" policy. The inference must be that O'Connell never drew a big following from well-to-do newspaper-reading Catholics. They were inclined to be conservative, and frightened of him.

Barrett and Haydn were only two of the many "characters" who drifted in and out of journalism in this period, some of them most entertaining in their eccentricities. There was the extraordinary Watty Cox, for example, who had made his name in the '98 period by editing a newspaper so scurrilous that the United Irishmen thought it must be printed in the Castle to justify reprisals. When the Castle offered a reward for the capture of the editor, Cox went and claimed it himself. A few years later he began publishing his *Irish Magazine*, the only periodical in these years that shows any originality. For the greater part of its life it was edited from Newgate Jail, where Cox was kept until the Government gave him a lump sum and persuaded him to leave for America. He was soon back, and publishing more squibs, but he was never the same force again. There was 'Honest Jack Lawless', who strove hard with newspapers and periodicals to keep liberalism alive in the North; and John Giffard, the man who is supposed to have coined the phrase "Protestant Ascendancy", who strove equally hard to keep Orange bigotry alive in the South. Then there is a whole field of research waiting to be done in the provincial newspapers. It took them a long time to recover from the '98 period, when they were all scooped into the Castle net with the help of threats or subsidies; but some of them would certainly repay study. The same is true of a little outcrop of trade union papers in Dublin around the time of the Reform Bill; they are still preserved in the British Museum. So also, is the *Dublin Times*—the first newspaper, so far as I know, of its kind—which cost the subscriber nothing—nought pence a copy. The idea was to get by on advertising alone, but for some reason it did not work, and the paper soon ceased publication.

But more important, perhaps, than the stories of individual newspapers is the history of something that was to affect *all* newspapers very greatly: the growth of the Trade Union movement. It happens that in this period the relations between employer and worker began to settle down into the pattern we now know to-day, with employers' association on the one hand and trade union on the other. Trade unions—or "combinations", as they used to call them then—had been known for a long time: the Statute Book in the eighteenth century is full of laws against them. But in some trades—particularly in the printing trade—the unions survived, and gradually struggled to a position where they were recognised, at least unofficially, by employers. The first cases of printing trade strikes that I have come across were in 1825. One of them concerned an *Irish Times*—no relation to the present one—which found itself in financial difficulties. It tried changing its name and making staff economies; but the staff reacted by downing tools, and, although there was a settlement, the paper soon afterwards collapsed. The other case was more serious. Richard Lonergan of the Dublin *Morning Post* had a dispute with his men about the ratio of apprentices to workers; and when the men went on strike, he put in some non-Union substitutes. On the night of February 27th, 1825, Lonergan and his men were crossing over Carlisle (O'Connell) Bridge when they were waylaid by strikers armed with bludgeons, and two men were injured. The strikers were prosecuted, but it was difficult to get evidence against them; they were only bound over. Such incidents led, however, to a general realization of the strength of the Unions; and in 1838 they had their first real official recognition when they were invited to give evidence before a Royal Commission. The Printers' Union Secretary claimed that the Union was primarily a friendly society to protect its members from unscrupulous employers and to pay unemployment relief—7s 6d. a week. But the employers claimed that the Unions were going far beyond this and trying to dictate such matters as apprenticeship: they were even demanding maximum hours of work and a minimum wage. Michael Staunton revealed that there had actually been a strike threat, to which he had given way, for shorter hours (the hours at that time were twelve a day). The most entertaining evidence came from Finlay, of the *Northern Whig*. When his men had threatened to go on strike he had gone to the local county school and brought back children, in secret, to teach them how to print his newspaper. He told the Commission:

"I slept the children upon the premises, and fed them upon the premises, and privately at night I took them out to give them exercise and air. I attended to their teaching myself; and by the time this strike came

I had these little boys taught—some, not more than ten years of age, whom I perched upon stools, and thus set at defiance the threats of these mighty combinators."

These "combinators", incidentally, counter-attacked by alleging that the employers had formed themselves into an association—a "ring", it would be called to-day —which was also illegal at the time. Finlay of the *Whig* unguardedly boasted of his agreements with other Belfast newspaper owners. The Chairman of the Royal Commission, gently reminded him that this was against the law. Ah, no! said Finlay: he never entered into any *written* contract!

One more instance may be given, also from the 1830's. The Trades Political Union, a Dublin organisation pledged to support the workers' cause, decided to publish a newspaper called the *People*. But a section of the T.P.U. broke away and denounced the venture, partly because the new paper was to be printed at the office of a reactionary newspaper, but mainly because it was to be printed by machinery; and that would mean that printers would be put out of work. In a powerful speech the editor-designate of the new paper forecast with surprising accuracy the immense expansion of employment that machinery would make possible in the newspaper business. But nobody paid any attention to him.

And finally, we come to the Young Ireland period. I do not propose to say anything about the papers which came out in the rebellion period itself, which I have not yet studied sufficiently closely: instead, I would like to say one or two things about the Young Ireland newspaper—the greatest newspaper in this country's history, and in its way, one of the most remarkable papers in the whole history of the press—the *Nation*.

When I began to work on the newspapers of the early

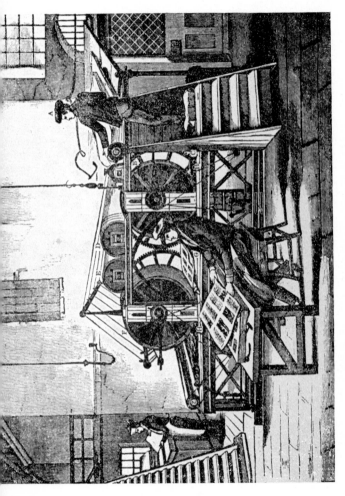

PRINTING PRESS, DUBLIN PENNY JOURNAL

1840's, I was half afraid that it might become clear that the *Nation's* influence had been inflated, exaggerated, expanded into myth and legend. Not at all. Its impact was astonishing. As I have mentioned during the earlier part of the century any newspaper which had one thousand readers was thankful. Three thousand was about the highest total reached—and that by a Protestant paper the *Evening Mail*. Yet the *Nation,* within a few weeks, had climbed to a circulation of ten thousand—large even by English standards. It was not a popular paper in the modern sense. No concessions were made to sensationalism, or anything of that kind. And it cost about the present day equivalent of *4s. 6d.* to buy. Yet it caught the public imagination as no other paper has done before or since. Why? If I had to sum up its virtue in a word, I would point to its integrity. Gavan Duffy, John Blake Dillon and especially Thomas Davis were men of honesty of purpose. They were not in the journalistic game to make money out of it or to win for themselves easy popularity. They would not trim, either to Ascendancy on the one side or O'Connell on the other, out of expediency. And just as you often know that integrity is embodied in a person merely by hearing them talk, so the public seemed to sense its presence when they read the *Nation,* and to like it. You know the old print of the cottagers crowding round the fireside to hear the *Nation* read to them? It is a sentimental picture; but I do not think it is a false one. The *Nation* revived something of the Irish tradition which was worth reviving. That some of it has been preserved since, is largely because of the influence the *Nation* had, not only in its own time, but on future generations. Many newspapers have been more famous, and some more influential, but none that I know had more nobility.

VIII

TRAVEL

BY KEVIN B. NOWLAN

WRITING AS LATE as the year 1842, an observant German traveller, J. G. Kohl, could comment that, "A man must travel a long way by railroad in England, or had best make up his mind to cross over to Ireland at once, if he wishes to see the antique stage coach offices which formerly abounded" in England. Travel methods and travel conditions were slow to change in Ireland. For one thing the Industrial Revolution was conspicious here by its absence outside of the north-east corner of country. The new industrial communities in the midlands and north of England could afford and demanded quicker and more efficient means of communication than the eighteenth century had known. The stage coach, by the eighteen-forties, was being pushed off the main routes and its place was being taken by the railway locomotive, the first real advance in transport for hundreds of years.

The effect of these developments in nineteenth century Britain, was to make Ireland, with its decaying industries and under-capitalised agriculture, something of a backwater in transport matters. But it would be wrong to suppose that there were no advances in the opening decades of the nineteenth century in Ireland. The contrary was the case. The rate of progress was, however, slow, and always somehow dogged by a want of the necessary money to do things properly. All this made for picturesque travel, the kind of thing which made a journey through Ireland something of an adventure for the visitor, but it did not always ensure comfort or speed. However, even at the beginning of the century, the traveller with money could get around Ireland safely enough, provided he was prepared for travel by a wide variety of vehicles, and had time and patience to spare.

How did people travel about the country in the years following the passing of the Act of Union? There were, of course, the Royal Mail coaches, operated by Post Office contractors, and maintaining a definite schedule. By mail coach it was possible to travel from Dublin to Cork, or Belfast or to a number of other provincial centres like Longford, Sligo and Waterford. But the mail and stage coaches were comparatively few in numbers, and the service infrequent. The result was that considerable tracts of country were left without public transport of any kind. Describing the conditions which existed in the opening years of the century, Charles Bianconi, of whom more later, said: "a farmer living twenty or thirty miles from his market town, spent the first day in going there, a second day in doing his business, and a third day in returning." For the man without horses, that long journey on foot could be a slow and possibly costly affair indeed.

But the stage coaches, where they did run, could travel quickly enough. In appearance they were similar to those great vehicles we can still see in old English coaching prints—with accommodation for passengers, both inside and outside, the latter places being, naturally, somewhat cheaper. With more respect than affection a traveller once described the Irish coaches as follows: "The carriages, though as solid as iron and steel can make them, are of surprising lightness, the horses swift as birds, and the coachmen artists in their line; but convenient seats you must not hope for, nor will you find it advisable to carry much luggage with you; all you have a right to expect is that wet or dry, clean or dirty, with whole bones or broken, you will be brought to the end of your journey within a few minutes of the appointed time."

The stage coaches, especially the day coaches, could undoubtedly travel fast. For example, about 1824, it was possible to leave Dublin, by coach, at 9 a.m. and arrive in Carlow at 2.30 p.m. on the same day, having travelled via Naas, Kilcullen, and Castledermot. And the fare? Coach travel was by no means cheap in Ireland. That journey from Dublin to Carlow cost 8s. 4d. for the passenger who decided to sit in the cramped carriage, or 5s. for the one who was prepared to sit outside, high up on the roof, and experience both the weather and the view. When allowance is made for the change in the value of money since 1824, the charge of 5s. single for an outside seat is quite a lot. Such a fare would make coach travel too expensive for a very large proportion of the population. It must be remembered that in the years before the Great Famine, the small farmer and cottier seldom handled money. Rents were frequently settled in terms of so many days work. And if a labourer were lucky enough to earn a shilling per day, the coach ride from Carlow to Dublin would cost him his week's wages. The stage coaches were for the middle-classes, and those of the gentry who did not choose to travel by horse or private car or post-chaise. The migratory labourer making his way to some seaport, the small farmer or dealer going to the next village or town, tramped it, or if the journey were not too long, went by one of those rather primitive carts the slightly better off farmers possessed.

The poverty of the people, the compartive absence

of large commercial or industrial centres and the high cost of travel, all combined to keep the stage coaches on the few main routes, and made travel—for the ordinary person—outside of a radius of a few miles of his native place, something to be undertaken only for some very special reason.

The late eighteenth century had seen in Western Europe a remarkable growth of interest in inland waterways as a means of bulk transport. With the growth in the population of towns, the roads in the more populous countries proved increasingly inadequate for the needs of commerce. The first phase of industrialisation in Britain, too, made the waterways of first-rate importance in the pre-railway era. A network of canals was created and rivers were deepened so as to link together the mining and industrial towns and to open new routes to the seaports and London. The period of canal construction in Britain reached its climax in the years between 1790 and 1830. Though the Irish main roads appear to have been better surfaced than the English ones which had to carry so much heavy traffic, Ireland was not unaffected by this new enthusiasm for waterways, and many people saw in the canals a means of opening up the resources of the countryside. With parliamentary assistance, not merely were rivers like the Boyne, Lagan and Barrow made navigable, but the task of opening the Shannon to through-traffic was undertaken, while the most outstanding achievements in canal construction were the Grand and Royal Canal systems.

In the first half of the nineteenth century, the Irish canals presented a much more animated picture than they did later in the century or indeed to-day. With the stage coaches so few in numbers, the canals carried not merely goods, but offered as well, a pleasant reasonably comfortable and fast passenger service across the middle of the island to the River Shannon.

The canal companies ran two kinds of passenger boats, a fast day boat, usually called a "fly boat", and a much slower and cheaper night service which was patronised by the poorer traveller, though on both day and night boats there was a strict division into first and second classes.

The fly boats or "swift passage boats" on the Grand Canal had a rather singular appearance. Drawn by two or three horses at a gallop they were extremely narrow in the beam, so much so that one traveller complained: "there is scarcely space to turn in the confined cabin". The boats were about thirty-five feet long, the roof of the cabin forming a small promenade deck. The room for the principal passengers, as it was called, had cushioned seats and large windows, while a very special feature of canal travel seems to have been the excellent meals that were served, despite the confined space.

Sir John Carr, the author of the *Stranger in Ireland* (published in 1806), assures us that the fly boat passengers could have "an excellent dinner on board, consisting of a leg of boiled mutton, a turkey, ham, vegetables, porter and a pint of wine each, at four shillings and tenpence a head." Not merely did the companies provide good meals, but the Grand Canal Company maintained comfortable hotels at the principal points along the canal. A fine example of a canal hotel, incidentally, is still to be seen at Portobello, Dublin.

In 1843, it was possible to travel from Dublin to Mullingar, on the Royal Canal, at a cost of 5s. 6d. first class, or 3s. second class. The distance was covered in good time. The boat left Dublin at 9 a.m. and arrived in Mullingar at 4.30 p.m. covering some fifty-two miles in seven and a half hours. The longer journey from Dublin to the Longford terminus was made in the heavier, slower night boat, which left Dublin at 2 p.m. and got to Longford at 8.15 the next morning, and the cost was —first class 9s. 5d., and second class 6s. 3d., exclusive, of course, of meals. The Grand Canal too, provided services between Dublin and Shannon Harbour, and passenger boats also travelled the branch canals to Athy, and across the Shannon to Ballinasloe. By "Swift Passage Boat" Shannon Harbour could be reached in eleven hours from Portobello at a cost of 11s. first class, and 7s. 6d. second class, though if the passenger wished to go on to Ballinasloe, by night boat, he could make the whole journey from Dublin for only 6d. more than the cost of the daytime journey to Shannon Harbour.

By the eighteen-forties the canal services had become closely integrated with the other transport facilities. Public cars going to Boyle, Co. Roscommon, for example, met the passenger boats at Longford, while at Shannon Harbour passengers could transfer to the Shannon Navigation Company's paddle steamers for the journey down the Shannon to Limerick. It was possible to make the journey Dublin to Limerick by inland waterways for a total cost of 16s. first class, or 11s. 4d. second class, not unreasonable prices by nineteenth century standards.

I have already mentioned Sir John Carr's praise of canal boat food, and to judge from the Royal Canal Company's notices, the management was particularly proud of the menu it had on offer, though, in strict accord with early nineteenth century principles, a sharp distinction was made between how much a gentleman could eat and drink, and the capacity and pocket of the humbler second class passenger. In 1843, a first class passenger could have breakfast with eggs for 1s. 3d. The second class, with egg in the singular, was only expected to pay 10*d*. Dinner for the first class cost 2*s*., but the poorer man paid as little as 1*s*. 3*d*. It was, however, in the matter of wine and spirits that the sharpest distinction was made. While a handsome dinner allowance of a naggin of spirits, or a half naggin of spirits and a half pint of wine, was made to each gentleman in the first class—the ladies were entitled only to the free wine —it was not deemed prudent to sell wine and spirits at all to the second class passengers. They had to remain content with bottled porter, at 5*d*. the bottle. The canal authorities, like many of their contemporaries, may have believed that temperance was really a matter of class distinction; good for the poor, but not so necessary for the wealthy.

The river Shannon, linked by canal with Dublin, had obvious advantages as a highway in the pre-railway age, but the course of the river was, unfortunately, hindered by rapids which reduced its value for transport purposes. Through the Board of Works public funds had been made available for the improvement of the river, but the work proceeded much too slowly. In consequence, it was impossible in the eighteen-forties to make an uninterrupted passage on the one boat from Shannon Harbour to Limerick. The paddle-steamer went as far as Killaloe, but as one traveller tells us: "Beyond Killaloe we came again to rocks and whirlpools, and as the canal was not yet finished . . . we had the amusement of landing with bag and baggage, and proceeding with jaunting cars to the spot where it was possible to embark for Limerick. The captain of the steamer and his mates shipped themselves on the backs of some cantering nags, and, thus caparisoned, rattled away in front as commanders and escort to the caravan. At the end of a few miles, we embarked again, but this time in a long canal boat drawn by a couple of horses."

So far we have been considering only public transport. But for the traveller whose journey took him away from the stage coach and canal routes—especially in the first two decades of the century—the private hire cars proved an absolute necessity. The first impression the Irish cars made on the stranger was the novelty of their appearance. The ubiquitous jaunting or outside car, in particular, aroused much comment, and sometimes amusement or annoyance as well. But there were other strange vehicles to be seen. A foreign traveller arriving at Kingstown, as it was then called, tells how he set out in a conveyance for Dublin. "It was a kind of square box, with glasses in the front, and we entered from behind. The machine went upon two wheels, and resembled some of the Chinese equipages of which I have read." This was clearly one of those high covered cars in which, we are told, the passenger sacrificed the view of the countryside for protection against the elements.

The lighter outside cars, were, however, in most general use. Cars and drivers were to be had in most towns and villages, though in some of the more remote parts of the country, especially in the west, difficulties could be experienced in finding either cars in reasonable repair, or the necessary horses.

To judge from the accounts, and prints, the Irish outside-car bore a close enough resemblance to the jaunting car still to be seen in some of our resorts. The wheels were, however, much smaller and the cars frequently longer than the more modern vehicles. The cars had, in some ways, much to commend them. The German traveller, J. G. Kohl, pointed out that with an outside car the visitor "is not bound to any particular line of road, and may travel whither he will, so he pay but his sixpence a mile; and then, as his feet are never far from the ground, he can step on and off at all times with very little trouble . . ."

There was, however, at least one serious disadvantage. On a jaunting car, the passenger was but slightly protected against the weather, and this was a difficulty which Charles Bianconi never succeeded in overcoming when he adopted a type of jaunting car for his public car service. What his friend, the artist, Michael Angelo Hayes, has to say about travel on a Bianconi car, in the rain, would apply equally well to the humbler jaunting car where indeed the protection might have been considerably less. He says, "In wet weather there were some inconveniences, it is true. The cars were provided with large oilcloth aprons, which protected the knees and came up almost as high as the chest, but these aprons afforded no shelter from the drippings of an umbrella. But worse still was the dreadful state of the cushions in wet weather. At times the passengers used literally to be sitting in a pool of water." According to Hayes, Bianconi tried to improve the position by having strips of wood placed "lengthways on the seats under the cushions, so that the water remained in the interstices and the cushions were kept fairly dry."

Despite the inconvenience, travel by hired private cars was not particularly cheap, and the hired car was essentially a luxury which only the better-off could enjoy. If the car were taken as a post-chaise when speed was essential, the horses were changed at fairly regular intervals and the cost could then be as much as 1s. per mile, while the drivers expected a gratuity of 3d. per mile in addition.

The nineteenth century saw, in the course of a comparatively short time, not merely a revolution in the means of transport, but also in the kind of people who travelled, and the number involved. The most important development was, of course, the railway. But if the railway made the excursion and the workman's ticket social facts, there were other more modest efforts to give the people cheap transport, that deserve to be noticed. Not the least interesting of these was Charles Bianconi's highly successful public car service which he built up in the years after 1815 with Clonmel as his headquarters.

Bianconi had come as a boy to Ireland from his north Italian home. As a humble dealer in coloured prints and frames he travelled about the countryside, and learned by experience that the poor man's carriage was his own two feet. He saw that a cheap, regular car service, running between the market towns and catering for the needs of the farmers and small merchants, was a venture well worth while attempting.

Profiting by the plentiful supply of good strong horses after the Napoleonic wars, Bianconi set up his first line in 1815. The beginning of what was to become a great undertaking was a service between Clonmel and Cahir. By carrying mails for local postmasters at low rates and by proving the regularity and cheapness of his cars, Bianconi quickly established his lines as the most efficient in the south of Ireland, and far more important for the travelling public than the stage coaches.

Speaking to the British Association for the Advancement of Science, in 1843, Bianconi could boast that, "I have now cars running from Longford to Ballina and Belmullet . . . from Athlone to Galway and Clifden . . . from Limerick to Tralee and Caherciveen . . ." The extent of the service may be judged from the fact that, in 1845, the "Bians"—as his cars were often called— covered some three thousand two hundred and sixty-six miles daily.

The delay in bringing the railways to Ireland made Bianconi's fortune. He built his own cars and had two principal types on the road, a two wheeler, and the long car, a four wheeler, capable of holding between sixteen and twenty passengers. From about 1833 onwards Bianconi tended to go over more and more to the long cars drawn by three or four horses, but the construction of both kinds of car was substantially the same. Only the size varied. The "Bian" was essentially a well-built, well-painted Irish outside car, and, by 1843, there were one hundred of them on the roads.

By paying his drivers, who were highly skilled men, a good wage, and by using only the best horses, Bianconi made his cars both fast and safe. The estimated average speed of a "Bian" was eight to nine miles per hour, and the fare per mile was as little as $1\frac{1}{2}d$. A Bianconi "Royal Mail and Day Cars" time-table is an impressive thing to see, and by all accounts it was a time-table that meant something in practice—for the astute Italian employed spies, who travelled as passengers, to report on the behaviour and performance of his drivers and local agents.

The Bianconi cars, despite their efficiency, however, had, in time, to give way before the advance of the railways. But their proprietor did not try to offer a futile opposition to the new ways in transport, and so in the last phase of their existence, in the eighteen-fifties and sixties, the Bianconi cars provided "feeder lines" to the railways or else brought public transport, for the first time, to remote places in the west and the north-west of the country.

The success of the Bianconi enterprise, with its depots in Clonmel, Sligo and Galway is, in itself a tribute to the honesty of the Irish countryside. The poor, rack-rented peasantry may have enforced a law of their own against landlords and agents, but their respect for the property and person of the traveller was impressive.

116

Car Travelling in the South of Ireland in the year 1856. Beaconis Establishment.

THE ARRIVAL AT WATERFORD. COMMINS HOTEL.

A BIANCONI CAR.

Speaking in 1857, towards the end of a long career, Bianconi could say, "My conveyances . . . have been travelling during all hours of the day and night . . . and during the long period of forty-two years that my establishment is now in existence, . . . the slightest injury has never been done by the people to my property, or that entrusted to my care . . ." Bianconi's words are confirmed by the police reports, for even in the most distressed times, highway robbery was not a common offence in nineteenth century Ireland.

The opening of the Stockton and Darlington Railway, in 1825, like the perfecting of the new spinning machines or the lighting of streets with coal gas, was an expression of the achievements and the needs of the new industrial urban age. The Industrial Revolution was not one triumphant procession. It brought with it its own social problems, and economic difficulties. But on the balance, the service it did was greater than its defects. It meant, in the long run, a higher standard of living for the ordinary person. Britain was the first country to prosper through the new industrial techniques, and Britain had, as a consequence the first railways.

Compared with many other European countries, the railway came to Ireland at an early date, but unfortunately the Irish economy, in pre-famine times, lacked that buoyancy necessary to make railway investment an attractive proposition for the private investor. Sustained state assistance might have led to more rapid expansion of the railway system, but successive British governments failed to free themselves completely from the narrow influences of current economic theories, and so railway construction in Ireland languished in the eighteen-thirties and forties. Only for lines along the East coast and in the vicinity of cities like Dublin and

Belfast was private capital forthcoming in any quantity. The real advances in railway construction followed the passing of the 1847 Railway Act. Under pressure of famine conditions, the government abandoned to some extent its objections to state interference in railway development, and some £600,000 was made available to the railway promoters.

The first Irish railway, with steam locomotives, was the Dublin and Kingstown Railway. The line was a short one, but from its opening, in 1834, it proved popular with the citizens of Dublin, and helped to open up the coastal district to the south of the city for residential purposes. The little suburban line, however, served to emphasise the almost unchallenged supremacy of the horse in Irish transport. In 1842, eight years after the opening of the first Irish railway, the only other in operation was the Ulster Railway from Belfast to Lurgan and Portadown which was built primarily to facilitate communications between the growing industrial port of Belfast and the market areas of western Ulster and Connacht.

SAOL AGUS CULTÚR IN ÉIRINN
IRISH LIFE AND CULTURE

The following booklets have been published in this series: